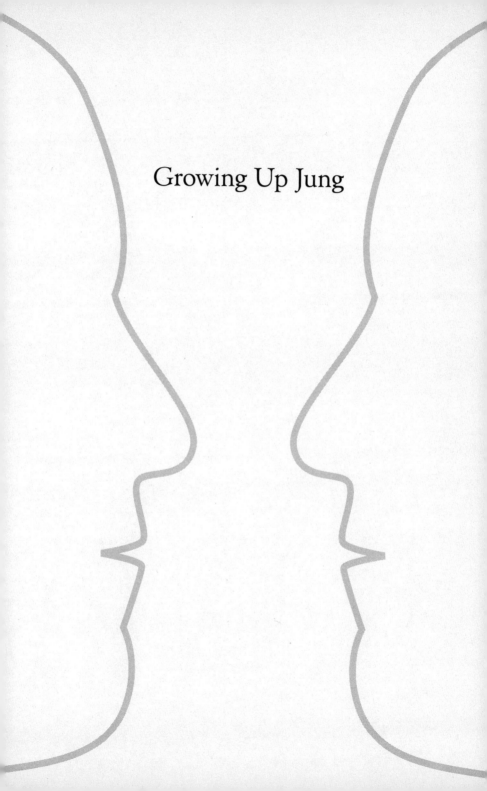

Growing Up Jung

Growing Up Jung

Coming of Age

as the Son of

Two Shrinks

Micah Toub

W. W. NORTON & COMPANY

New York · London

For information about permission to reproduce selections from this book, write to Permissions, W. W. Norton & Company, Inc., 500 Fifth Avenue, New York, NY 10110

For information about special discounts for bulk purchases, please contact W. W. Norton Special Sales at specialsales@wwnorton.com or 800-233-4830

Manufacturing by Courier Westford
Book design by Chris Welch
Production manager: Anna Oler

Library of Congress Cataloging-in-Publication Data

Toub, Micah.
Growing up Jung : coming of age as the son of two shrinks / Micah Toub.
p. cm.
Includes bibliographical references.
ISBN 978-0-393-06755-2 (hardcover)
1. Jungian psychology. 2. Individuation (Psychology) 3. Toub, Micah.
4. Psychoanalytic interpretation—Case studies. I. Title.
BF175.T68 2010
150.19'54092—dc22
[B]

2010006315

W. W. Norton & Company, Inc.
500 Fifth Avenue, New York, N.Y. 10110
www.wwnorton.com

W. W. Norton & Company Ltd.
Castle House, 75/76 Wells Street, London W1T 3QT

1 2 3 4 5 6 7 8 9 0

For my family

Contents

Introduction 11

1. The Marginalized *A Terrorist in the Family* 15

2. Dreambody *The Volcano on My Father's Nose* 43

3. The Oedipus Complex *My Mother's Small Lover* 69

4. Anima *Getting Laid the Jungian Way* 106

5. Relationship *Synchronicity and the Meaning of Love* 134

6. The Shadow *My Archetypal Lust for Violence* 162

7. The Ally *A Spirit Guide in the Suburbs* 189

8. Individuation *The Elusive Conclusion* 224

Acknowledgments 255

Notes 257

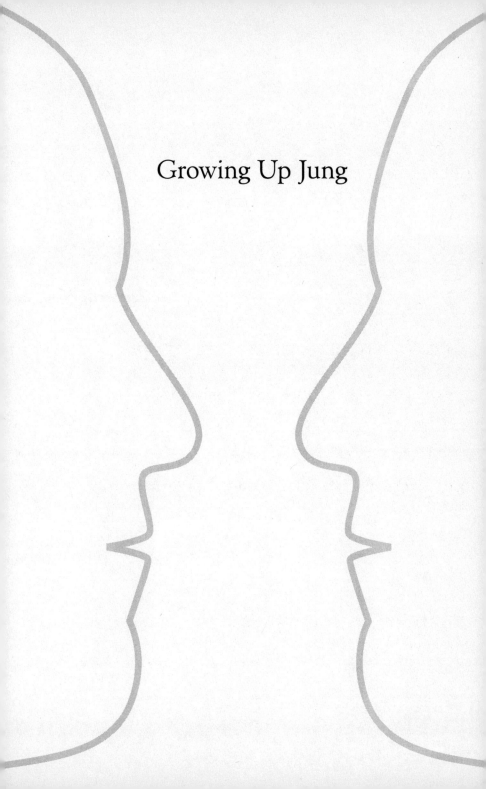

Growing Up Jung

Introduction

"Did you have a dream last night?" my father asked me. We were sitting in the car, waiting for my mother and sister. I was four years old.

"Yes," I said, though I hadn't had one or, if I did, I couldn't remember it. "I was underground and I was in a machine that could travel through the earth."

"Wow, that's really interesting, Micah," he said in his genuinely interested tone of voice. "And then what happened?"

I tried to imagine more clearly the dream scene I was describing—a cross section of the earth, with me in a small, metal, drill-like vehicle plowing ahead into all the brown mud under the surface. I wasn't sure what would happen next if this were a real dream. The anxiety made it hard to decide, but just before I thought my father might start to get suspicious, I had it. "I was being chased by a monster," I said really fast, breathing a secret sigh of relief. "A giant worm that can also travel through the earth," I added. This was a very believable dream, I thought to myself. This was easy. You didn't even have to *have* dreams. You could just make them up.

"What did the monster look like?" he asked, eyeing me in his rearview mirror. "Did it say anything as it chased you?"

I wanted my father to like me, to be proud of me. A psychologist's son wants to have a grade-A psyche. But being the son of a psychologist also meant saying exactly what you were thinking and feeling—it meant telling the truth. And my duty to honesty was now in conflict with my desire for him to be impressed by my dream. I had changed my mind. I now wanted to tell him the truth, that I didn't have a dream about being chased by an earth-burrowing monster and didn't remember my dream at all. But it was too late.

"I don't remember the rest," I said.

"Uh huh." My father nodded, turning his mouth into a thought-ful frown, which was his response for both skepticism and when his mind was heading into its Jung space, coming to analytical conclusions. This made it difficult to know whether he thought I was lying or had had a superior dream by Jungian standards. Just then, my sister Andreya opened the door and jumped in next to me. She saved me from ever finding out.

Archetypically, as a Jungian would say, my coming-of-age story is just like yours. But of course, on closer inspection, growing up as the son of two shrinks also involved some marked differences from what would be considered normal. When I was growing up, my parents often had their offices in the house, which, in my mind, meant that waves and waves of screwed up, crazy, lunatic weirdos were allowed to enter our altar of rational normalcy. I mean, I knew that in some ways my parents were different from most parents. Most people did not go off to seminars in the desert and sit cross-legged with a bunch of other people and talk about their spirit guides. But, I had decided, in spite of that, my family was a sane, psychologically intact family. And that made us different from the people who waited just inside the front entrance, on the other side of a thin wooden door which I pressed my ear to hoping to hear somebody talking to himself. (I assumed most of my dad's clients were schizophrenics—it's the most interesting *sounding* disorder in any case.) I never did hear any multiple-personality voices, but I heard the odd sigh, cough, or grunt, sounds into which I tried to read their sadness and angst.

I once passed one of my father's clients as I was coming around from the backyard and he was on his way up the front steps. The man's pants were splattered with paint, which is why I later called him The Artist. When he saw me come around, he looked me in the eyes and gave me a smile, the kind of smile that I swear spoke these words: "Hey kid, everyone in this crazy world is pretending to be normal, going on with all the bullshit, but you and I know what's really going on, don't we?" At the time, I joked to myself that telepathy must be a power that schizophrenics wielded. But the weird thing was, I thought he was onto something—I agreed with the man's smile. Maybe the two of us did know something no one else did.

I imagined The Artist sitting across from my father, telling him about how he had been working at a fast-food restaurant and was fired after a week because he refused to make fries to the standard of his shift manager. Also, I decided, he refused to take a shower and sometimes he didn't wear shoes. He didn't care if people thought he was crazy.

When I tell people that both my parents are psychologists, they usually raise an eyebrow. "Wow," they say, "but you're so well-adjusted," ironically assuming that having grown up under the microscope of analysis it's a miracle I do not have a dozen psychological disorders. Or do I, they ask—at which point I usually give them The Artist's smile.

And so, in the spirit of the psychology-padded nest from which I sprung, here are some of my stories, self-analyzed by this son of analysts through my own investigation into the ideas and concepts that my parents fed me as I grew from a boy into a man.

1

The Marginalized

(A Terrorist in the Family)

"Well, if you're just going to stare at the ceiling instead of making eye contact with me and won't tell me how you're feeling, why don't you describe what you see? Perhaps you see a figure or a story in the shapes of the plaster that will help us to know what's happening with you?"

My father said this in the fluffy-edged psychologist voice that he would have used with all his clients that week. It's marked by a soothing sound that begins far back in the throat and is followed by a series of slow, encouraging nods. I always knew that when he spoke like that to my sister things were not going well.

"I see a ceiling," Andreya said. "And I *don't* feel like talking about it."

I later dubbed this event, which occurred in the downstairs family room of our house, the Toub Family Peace Conference of

1986. I was ten years old; my sister, fourteen. We lived in a tract housing suburb of Denver, Colorado, so our family room was identical to the thousands of other family rooms in the thousands of other houses that expanded outward from ours in a seemingly never-ending and symmetrical grid. I can't help feeling, though, that what was happening that day, in our family room, was unique.

I viewed the proceedings from the kitchen, half a floor up, where I engaged my G.I. Joes in quiet battle on the linoleum floor. My father sat on one side of the long, red, velour couch and my sister leaned against the arm on the opposite side. My father wasn't a huge man, but he always maintained an athletic physique due to his weekly racquetball matches. Compared to Andreya, he was the physically dominant one, but he always undercut his muscular stockiness with a gentle demeanor that seemed, in its affect, to equalize the two of them. Andreya, with her half-black skin and curly brown hair—hair that she spent hours straightening every day to look more like the girls on television and in her school—didn't much resemble our father. Well, actually not at all. She is a child from our mother's first marriage; my father adopted her when she was three. Leaning toward her chin-first, my father was attempting to make eye contact with Andreya through his square-framed glasses. She refused to capitulate, shielding herself with her scowling dark eyebrows and arms across her chest. My mother, an ally to both parties, sat on the rocking chair on the other side of the room, her small frame swallowed by its plaid pattern. She had been a tireless mediator over the years, but now she was letting the negotiations take place without her involvement, trying to say nothing. There was very little light coming into the room since it was halfway underground, lending the event an ominous air.

My father let out a great sigh and shook his head slowly, sadly. I eyed the ceiling above their heads. The white mass of ridged plaster was a scorched and hopeless landscape of dunes. A prisoner, ankles tied, was being marched across the desert to his execution while, alongside, his captors rode a camel. An unidentified flying object hovered above the scene, observing. I wished that my sister would see these things too, but she wasn't even trying.

"Every family has a culture," my mother told me a few years ago, "and as in all cultures, whether it's a country or a company, there's a mainstream way of doing things—the way most people do them—and then there's a smaller group that doesn't do things that way. That group is the marginalized faction."

I nodded. We were discussing—and not for the first time—what had happened so that my father and sister were hardly speaking anymore and had had almost no relationship for fifteen years. We were analyzing the history of the struggle, trying to tease out the root causes and I could tell my mother was coming to a conclusion.

"We call that marginalized role in the group the *terrorist*. And Andreya," my mother said very gravely, "was the terrorist of our family."

The theory, she went on to explain, was something she learned from one of her first mentors, post-Jungian Arnold Mindell. At the time, she wasn't in contact with him much, but when I was growing up, she and my father were members of his inner circle and his psychological theories and practices had been a constant presence in our house. Back then, he was always just referred to as "Arny," but nowadays I like to refer to him as my parents' "former guru."

In my head, I created the movie: a family sitting around the dinner table—a Thanksgiving spread with turkey, stuffing, cranberry sauce, the works. They're all wearing knit sweaters and smiles. But if you peer beyond the table, into the darkness of the family room below, you can just make out a trench dug in the carpet, a teenager peeking above, her face smudged with dirt so as to be camouflaged with the brown shag. Her arm is cocked back, ready to pitch a grenade and take out the whole placid lot of them.

It sounds like an exaggerated illustration, but my mother would say that my scene is *exactly* what she's talking about. In fact, my mother never exaggerates, though she is prone to the use of metaphors. The scene, she would say, represents *what is really happening*.

The terrorist, she explained to me, acts in opposition to a family's prescribed way of being. The terrorist is the one who refuses to be involved in family rituals and doesn't laugh at the family jokes.

He is the black sheep, the one people are referring to when they say, "They're such a nice family, but that Joey, well, he's *different*, isn't he?"

In a wealthy, social-climbing family, this person might sell all his belongings and head off to Africa. If one's parents are artists, instead of being creative, eccentric, and persistently broke, the terrorist might become a clock-punching accountant with a spouse, two kids, and a dog. Like a family's signature odor, a family's culture may not always be something that's considered positive by the world outside the boundaries of that family's walls: "C'mon, Jimmy, have another beer. It's not going to kill you. Since when did my son become such a wuss?"

Sometimes, the marginalized member of the family actually appears to be in the mainstream by most people's standards. Alex P. Keaton, the Ronald Reagan–loving, money-grubbing son of two bleeding-heart liberals in *Family Ties*, was the terrorist of his television sitcom family.

However, even if the grenade-wielding daughter at Thanksgiving is an accurate picture of *what's really happening* emotionally, I figured that when Arny used the same term given to suicide bombers for a member of one's family, he meant only to hammer home his point. But, as I found out after stealing some of his books off my parents' shelves, this is not exactly the case.

As it turns out, Arny has worked not just with groups of hippies, but has also been a mediator in international conflicts that involved the kind of disputes and violence we normally associate with the term *terrorism*. In his book *Sitting in the Fire*, Arny suggests that alienation and anger, whether on the world scale, in companies, or in families and relationships, are in some ways parallel in their dynamics. The book is mostly written about working with political groups, but Arny writes that like these bigger groups, small groups like families also include members who are marginalized as a result of possessing qualities or attitudes that the mainstream system has shut out. In fact, he says the very existence of the terrorist comes about *because* certain qualities are repressed from the mainstream. The main thrust of Arny's book is that conflict arises in groups—between the terrorist and the mainstream, for example—from a need to shift the culture in a direction that is more inclusive and whole. Both the country and the family need to figure out how to integrate the terrorist's qualities and attitudes into the mainstream culture to make the terrorist role unnecessary. Therefore, one could consider his wayward sister akin to a suicide bomber and, at the same time, a suicide bomber could be viewed as a sister—a sister in a family in which she doesn't quite fit in, and who has taken up an unwelcome viewpoint simply because no one else did.

———————

Our family culture was a particularly calm and encouraging one. "That's *good* that I died in your dream, Micah," my father once told me. "That means you're integrating your inner father and becoming more independent."

We talked about our problems, and we understood that our issues with each other were often just issues within ourselves. "I am angry with you right now because the part of me represented by you is not being allowed to emerge into consciousness," we might say. "It's not you, it's me."

Self-reflection—or taking the *meta*view—was a highly valued trait and, even now, the fact that I'm writing this, stepping back to consider the concept of a family culture and applying it to my own family, is a direct result of that. And the fact that I just wrote that sentence raises me to an even higher plane—the meta-metaview. Reflecting on life in double-meta land is perhaps a bit, I don't know, self-indulgent, but in my family, it is a great achievement. Little practicalities like trimming the weeds in the backyard or buying a new kitchen table when the old one is falling apart are lower functions, and if you have time to get around to them, fine.

I often secretly visited my father's office when I was growing up, because it was usually located in the house. As a boy, I'd sit in the client's chair, which was unusually cushy and made of a dark red fabric as soft as velvet. I'd imagine my father sitting there across from me, the two of us talking about some very serious things. A box of Kleenex sat on a small wooden table to the side, one tissue straining to escape.

The walls were covered with magical and frightening pictures that represented past layers of my father's unconscious. He'd had an important dream about Robin Hood and so, for a while, drawings and paintings of Robin Hood colonized the office. Newer obsessions would come along and take over, but certain favorite pieces from each stage remained.

Old, tattered hardback books lined his shelves, including a whole row of those mysterious black ones by Jung with strange titles like *The Psychogenesis of Mental Disease* and *Mysterium Coniunctionis*.

On the small table next to my father's chair was a lined yellow notepad and one of the refillable pens that he always used. The notepad was blank, ready to be scribbled on with dream symbols, interpretations, reflections. I imagined him sitting there across from me, taking notes about what I was saying. I was sure that he would double underline certain things I said, because my psyche was *that* interesting. I wondered what he would write about me: "Micah is shy, has trouble making friends, but seems to possess an above-average intelligence. He occasionally suffers from delusions of grandeur (imagines that his life is a movie in which he is the hero). Appears to find gratification in being analyzed by his parents. Self-centered?"

Obviously, my sister didn't romanticize their profession as much as I did. She was the terrorist, after all. "Getting upset and holding a grudge was not allowed," my mother said, summarizing my family's culture. "So Andreya was marginalized."

The inciting incident that led to the Toub Family Peace Conference had occurred the previous week. For the amusement of her best friend who lived across the street, Andreya had made me walk through a pile of dog shit.

"Hey, Micah, do you want to see something really cool?" she had asked me. Cindy was standing next to her smiling like an angel. I, being gullible and desperate for attention from my sister, didn't question their motives.

"Yes," I said. "What is it?"

"We can't tell you, you just have to see it. Close your eyes," Andreya said and held out her hand to me. My sister never wanted to hold my hand. I gave it to her and grasped tightly.

I heard the screen door groan open. Then as I was being led forward, the sun hit my face. I was walking on the soft grass of our front yard, then onto the concrete of the sidewalk.

"Turn right," my sister said, so I did, quietly expectant.

Then she let go of my hand and the two of them burst into laughter. I kept my eyes closed because I had not yet been told to open them.

"You just stepped in dog poop!" her friend squealed. I opened my eyes and saw the flattened piece of poo behind me. I lifted my bare foot to see a yellowy smear on my skin. My sister turned her head down, shyly ashamed, but her friend was doubled over, cracking up. Tears flooded my eyes and I ran inside.

"You better not tell Mom and Dad!" my sister called after me. But I did, of course. I told on her.

Normally, my parents' solution to something like this would have been to have a "talk." The purpose of the talk would be to get to the root of the problem, to find out what was *going on* with Andreya. Things were never just what they were. No, something *was happening* and my parents would get to the bottom of it. Or not, as was the case with Andreya.

The questions: Was Andreya's disobedience a symptom of her unhappiness with the family dynamic? Was she acting out because she wasn't able to consciously communicate an emotion?

Her answer was: "I don't want to talk about it and you can't make me."

Andreya had always put up a wall whenever pressured to dialogue in this way and as she made her way into adolescence, the wall wasn't coming back down. She'd been hardly communicating with my parents at all, shunning my father in particular.

The dog poop incident had followed another, perhaps more serious, infraction. Andreya was caught coming home after sneaking out her window one night with a bottle of our parents' vodka under her arm.

In our family culture, like most, sneaking out of the house on a school night or walking your innocent, sweet and loving younger sibling through dog shit was grounds for punishment. But even worse than those acts of teen delinquency was refusing to talk about it. Not wanting to figure out what unconscious anger was behind such acts was a *serious* transgression.

Andreya was grounded for two weeks, which was the first time my parents had ever resorted to such a conventional punishment.

Dinner the day after was tense.

"How was school today?" my father asked Andreya.

Andreya acted as if nothing had been said, because to her my father didn't exist. I stabbed at my peas, silently praying that she would just say something.

"Come on. Just tell us one thing," he said.

My mother attempted to intervene. "Maybe she doesn't—"

"I'm just asking her a question. She doesn't *have* to talk if she really doesn't want to."

"School was *fine*," my sister said.

"Were you able to get help from your math teacher?"

"No."

"No? Andreya, you have to ask for help or you're never going to get your grade up."

"I *know*."

"So . . . are you going to do it tomorrow?"

"I don't know."

"Andreya—"

"Maybe she doesn't know what questions to ask," I interrupted.

I often acted as my sister's dinner-table defense attorney. Like my father, I couldn't understand why Andreya wouldn't want to do better in school, but I hated fights between them and it seemed like she needed help. She could express raw emotion better than any of us, but matching my father on logical grounds was not her strength.

"Micah, it's true that even asking the right questions takes some idea of what's going on, but you can always get a teacher to repeat something until you understand. Andreya should be talking to the teacher after class one-on-one."

Andreya's eyes darkened. I braced myself.

"Can we *please* talk about something else?" she said.

"No. I think we need to resolve this issue. Don't you?"

Silence.

"*Andreya* . . ."

"No."

My father took in a deep breath, then said something that was probably not from any of his psychology textbooks. "Well, I guess it's up to you. But if you don't start being more assertive with your education, you're going to end up stupid with no job!"

"Don't say that!" my mother shouted.

Andreya slammed down her fork and left the table.

Those two weeks passed slowly. No matter how much the rest of the family tried to pretend everything was okay, when Andreya was in a bad mood, it cast a darkness throughout the whole house. You could hear her silence emanating from her bedroom, and you could feel every word you spoke being hated by her.

But finally, the date of her release came, and the Toub Family Peace Conference was arranged. Being only a junior member of intrafamily affairs, I was not informed of the exact agenda, but it seemed to me that this was not simply a discussion of what to do about Andreya playing a prank on me or sneaking out of the house. It was more of a State of the Family deal and, specifically, was meant to examine the deterioration of the relationship between my father and my sister. Yes, this monumental occasion was going to take the whole, huge, ugly issue of the father-daughter conflict head on.

So there they were, my father asking—begging—my sister to look up at the ceiling and tell him what she saw, and my sister refusing to do it.

"Well," my father said, after the long silence, "if you won't talk to me, and you won't even tell me what you see in the ceiling, I'm going to just say what I'm thinking." Arny had always preached extreme in-the-moment honesty, even if it meant just taking a guess or saying the wrong thing, a directive my father had been trying to follow. "Or . . . really it's a feeling. Andreya, when you won't share with me the problems in your life, and enter into a discussion of how to solve them, I feel like you don't love me anymore."

My G.I. Joes on the yellow-tiled linoleum field of battle abruptly halted their combat. There was a brief moment of silence as Andreya's face reddened, and then came the explosion. "Maybe I don't!" she screamed, the words ricocheting off the wood paneling, followed by my sister dramatically storming to her bedroom, stomping her feet as hard as possible on the way. The splintering bang of her faux-oak door slamming shut was the loudest sound that was ever heard in that house.

It seems to me now that the problem between my sister and my father might have been my fault. Or rather, it might have been because I was born, which is not technically my fault, but the condom's. (I've been assured by my parents that they were "happy" when they found out I was on the way.)

To gain a greater understanding of how my parents might have learned to view sibling rivalry during their training, I went looking into Jung's books. I got quickly distracted, however, by a case study Jung shares in *The Development of Personality*, which details a three-year-old girl's reaction to the birth of her brother.

Besides inspiring the girl to coax the truth about sex and conception from her parents, the new baby also inspired in her a darker motive.

"On the evening before the birth," wrote Jung, "when labor pains were just beginning, the child found herself in her father's room. He took her on his knee and said, 'Tell me, what would you say if you got a little brother tonight?' 'I would kill him,' was the prompt answer."

Andreya did not try to kill me—not right away. Initially, she tried to breast feed me. I was told this story when I was very young and during the dark ages of her adolescence I used to think back on it to remind myself that she loved me and, in fact, had once loved me so much she wanted me to be *her* baby.

"But you wouldn't do it!" she reminds me to this day.

"I'm sorry!" I always reply.

"It's okay. I feel bad, though, because when you wouldn't do it I dropped you and hit you on the head."

"I know, and I forgive you."

"I got in major trouble from Mom and Dad for that. They wouldn't let me touch you for weeks."

My mother has told me that my father and Andreya were close before I was born. I've seen the faded photographs that prove it: my father, sporting a ponytail and a handlebar mustache, holding toddler Andreya; my father in the backyard watching as Andreya played with mud.

I never thought of her as my *half*-sister—she had been there since I was born. And while her *half* status became more apparent after I arrived and must have had something to do with her becoming the black sheep of the family, the fact is, her personality simply stood out in contrast to the rest of us.

In addition to being largely uninterested in academics within a family that based a large part of its identity around getting straight

A's, Andreya was a material girl in a family that didn't believe in such superficiality. Our house was furnished almost exclusively by other people's junk we'd found at garage sales, while Andreya had a lust for new things, the best things, and lots of things. And in a family devoted to conflict resolution, she wanted to stay angry and wasn't going to let my parents take that away from her.

The funny thing is, in the suburbs where we lived, Andreya's personality didn't stand out so much. The fact that she liked to own nice, new things was not exactly odd in late twentieth-century America. The fact that she wasn't crazy about New Age ideas in the early 1980s was certainly in sync with the way most people were feeling at the end of the "free love" decades.

Of all the inhabitants in the rows of houses of our suburb, where the backyards all lined up in one long, green stretch with wooden fences dividing them into equal plots, my mother was, I believe, the only adult who ever sunbathed nude. She did this despite the fact that the balconies of the houses on either side of us had clear sightlines into our backyard. And we were probably the only family on the block with Bob Marley blasting out of the stereo and whose family room on occasion took on the sweet scent of marijuana. In my second grade class, I was the only kid whose parents supported Mondale over Reagan, which I discovered when my construction paper cutout of a blue donkey was crushed beneath a pile of red elephants in our mock election. I can guarantee that my father was the only man in the area who practiced regular meditation. Of course, none of this was visible from the outside (save the nudism). My father owned a normal enough Jeep Cherokee, and headed off to work every morning. On his way to help clients use dream signs to navigate their true life paths, he looked just like any other dad heading off in his button-down shirt and slacks. Eventually, though, neighbors would ask what he did for a living and, sticking to his code of honesty, he would be forced to tell them. He once told me that after he'd reveal that he was a psychologist, they were always on guard about what they said to him, fearing that he would analyze them.

So if you take the metaview—as I like to do—my sister was the terrorist of our family, but our family was the terrorist of our neighborhood. Andreya was embedded, so to speak.

Throughout my childhood, I was sheltered from the cynic's opinion of Jung. Nobody ever said anything overly negative about him to my face. Not until just a few years ago, in fact.

"Jungian therapy is just a way for privileged, middle-class people to feel better about themselves. It's utterly useless to help people who have real problems," Helen felt compelled to tell me an hour after I'd arrived from out of town for a visit and had announced excitedly that I was going to write a book about growing up with Jungian parents. It takes a special friend to feel comfortable enough with you to challenge your parents' whole raison d'être.

Silence, I believe, was my response.

I didn't have a defense straight off because I hadn't ever really given it any thought. I'd always assumed that what my parents did for a living was useful, that it was worthwhile for people and even that they were performing an important service to all of humanity. My father had been a Jungian analyst since I was a baby and though my mother had followed him on the Jungian path a bit later in my childhood, that was still before I even understood what their jobs entailed, other than talking to people about their dreams.

Helen was earning her PhD in clinical psychology and had done some of her training at a hospital where people with "real problems"—schizophrenia and other serious mental disorders— came to get healed enough to function in a very basic way. She told me that no one studied Jung anymore in school.

"But Jung helps people uncover the mysteries of their unconscious," I said. She raised an eyebrow. I laughed sheepishly.

It struck me then that, in contrast to Helen's job, the Jungian technique of talking to relatively normal people about the mythological content of their dreams did seem kind of soft-focus. Helen deals with the people who don't choose to go into therapy and most of them couldn't afford to, regardless. A lot of them would be unable to function on a daily basis without the aid of medication and therapeutic support. Their problems are perhaps more pressing than those of a whining executive who needs help dealing with guilty feelings caused by having two mistresses.

"Your parents just make rich people feel okay about their lives," Helen repeated. And, presumably, I thought, okay about being rich.

Apparently, Jung had this very concern himself. According to Deirdre Bair's definitive biography of Jung, when his practice was taking off in the 1920s, his clients mainly consisted of middle-aged women, most of whom were rumored to be in love with him. Jung made wads of cash helping these women with their bourgeois anxieties. Collectively, they were sometimes referred to as the "Jungfrauen," which was a play on German words. *Frauen* means "women" but since *Jung* also meant "young" the whole word carries the meaning "virgin." So these women were Jung's virgins. Bair shares the words of a former patient of Jung's, who wrote in her diary that he'd complained later in life about the situation: "I never seemed to have an interesting patient, some scientific mind, some man of quality who had achieved something at least. Just the eternal line of spinsters. They arrived in droves; it never seemed to end. I used to ask myself 'why am I cursed?' But I plodded along, looking after them the best I could, doing my research work on the side."

Before becoming a student of psychology, Jung was just another cynic about his future profession. At university, Jung was equally interested in hard science as he was in religion and philosophy and agonized over which path to follow (in his memoir he describes at length possessing two personalities—he calls them No. 1 and No. 2—which went to battle over the decision). In the end, he studied medicine because he figured it would give him the best shot at a viable career.

It was while studying medicine that he first picked up a textbook on psychiatry, at the time a loathed profession. "I began with the preface, intending to find out how a psychiatrist introduced his subject or, indeed, justified his reason for existing at all," Jung wrote. He explains that his early disparaging attitude toward the field was due to the fact that both psychiatric patients and their doctors were locked away in isolation. Nobody heard much from them and the rumor was that the psychiatrist was sometimes as crazy as his patients. Meanwhile, mental disorders were largely unexplainable, so were generally avoided by those in medical school who wanted to have an easy, successful career. But, while reading, Jung came across the phrase "diseases of the personality," and something clicked in him. His heart started racing, and he realized "that for me the only possible goal was psychiatry." He'd still harbored an interest in philosophy and metaphysical matters, and psychiatry, he wrote, "at last was the place where the collision of nature and spirit became a reality."

After graduating, and suffering from ribbings from his medical school buddies, Jung obtained his formative position at the Burghölzli Mental Hospital in Zurich in 1900. It was the same year that Freud published *The Interpretation of Dreams*, though the friendship and professional alliance between the two wouldn't begin until six years later. At the hospital, Jung was charged to make the rounds to hundreds of patients, taking detailed notes by hand on the status of each one. He often felt frustrated that he did not have more time with them, but he started to do something that was unheard of up until then: he talked to patients as if they were "normal" people, asking them about their personal stories. Through these dialogues and running association tests, Jung came to be able to work with patients who had schizophrenia, known then as dementia praecox.

It was at this time that Jung and Freud first read each others' work and realized they shared a belief in the unconscious, and had similar methods for discovering the unconscious motives behind psychosis and neurosis. They bonded quickly—at one point Freud even referred to Jung as the "crown prince" of psychoanalysis—

but their cooperation was destined to last for only about six years when, finally, Jung became interested in mythology and meta-physics, a direction Freud scorned.

It seemed, from what Helen was saying, academia agreed in the end with Freud's judgment.

"Helen, you're on the front lines. Somebody needs to be on the front lines. But Jungian therapy helps people more on a spiritual level." This was Helen's husband, William, also an old friend of mine, coming to my defense.

Helen rolled her eyes. "Maybe," she said, "but I'm just saying, there isn't even any proof that Jungian therapy works."

"Everybody needs a different kind of therapist," I countered. "And it's more about the bond with the therapist that is important."

"But nobody has ever tried to collect data to prove it even helps people," she said finally.

I kept debating, trying different angles to defend Jungian analysis, but in the back of my head I did wonder: Were my parents just the psychological oil of the bourgeois?

The first time I met Arny was in the early 1980s at a large cabin in the Rocky Mountains, a few hours away from where we lived. It was a weekend retreat seminar he ran, which was attended by around twenty people, including my parents.

I remember Arny as a shape shifter, in one minute a mischievous clown capable of a thousand facial expressions and then, in the next, a stern sergeant in command of any room he occupied. He'd carry himself with the ethereal detachment of the Buddha, and then suddenly would peer hawklike into your eyes and say hello to your naked soul. As a young boy I was equal parts intrigued and frightened. Also, Arny seemed rarely to be wearing a shirt.

My sister and I were the only kids at the seminar, but nobody minded us being there. In fact, I once caught some of the adults huddled around a window, watching me as I ran around, pretending to chase down Russian spies in the forests of Siberia. I waved awkwardly when I saw them and then retreated deeper into the woods. (My father later told me that observing me had helped them all contact their inner children.)

When I was tired I'd go inside and sit down next to my parents, who were gathered with everyone else in a big circle in the main room. The scenes I saw in that circle are a blur of participants dancing in slow motion accompanied by high-pitched wails, gripping each other's forearms like Sumo wrestlers, barking out random swear words and nonsensical insults at each other. It was all a part of Process Work, Arny's very own splinter sect of Jungian psychology.

Arny started off as a student of physics at MIT, where he was drawn especially to the then-newly-discovered and unexplained world of quantum physics. It was an interest that led him to Zurich, Switzerland, where, as an exchange student, he says he was "trying to follow the path of Albert Einstein" who had also studied in that city. Arny arrived in 1961, coincidentally a week after Jung's death.

In Zurich, Arny started to have some wild dreams. When he told a friend about them, the friend suggested that Arny go into Jungian analysis. He did, and shortly thereafter, Arny had a dream where Jung told Arny what his life's purpose was.

"Well, Arny, don't you know what your job in life is?" Jung said to him in the dream. "Well, the job that you have in your life is to find the connections between psychology and physics." Not knowing much about psychology, Arny was skeptical of the idea. At the time, Arny says he didn't think dreams were very important and was more interested in what could be observed in what he later called "consensus reality." But the dream and Jung's words stayed with him, he stayed in analysis, and enrolled at the Jungian Institute in Zurich in addition to continuing his studies in physics. After receiving a diploma from the Institute, he completed his PhD in psychology back in the United States, and, soon after, Jung's prophesy in Arny's dream became a reality. Arny developed a new therapeutic practice called Process Work, which asks that you examine everything that occurs in your life—especially what occurs in the physicality of your body or in the surrounding environment—as a manifestation of the unconscious. Jung looked at dreams for this, but Arny felt that you should also look at that pain in your ear, persistent headaches, or the energy that seems to be coming from the broom standing in the corner of the room as guiding messages.

Arny, influenced by Eastern philosophy, views everything as essentially connected, so that everything that surrounds us holds a possibility for finding meaning and direction. My father urging my sister to look at the ceiling and describe what she sees was inspired by this philosophy. Of course, this kind of practice is reminiscent of age-old psychological tests like Dr. Rorschach's inkblots. Process Work takes it a step further, though. Instead of simply describing the inkblots, Arny would ask you to *become* the inkblot. How would the inkblot move? What would the inkblot say?

And so the political conflict in my family was solidified. On the one side were my parents, wielding their psychological techniques. On the other side was my sister, who didn't want to have anything to do with those techniques or, increasingly, anything to do with my parents at all. Of course, my parents' idea of working out the schism with Andreya was to use those same psychological techniques that my sister wanted nothing to do with. And the big surprise is—finally—it didn't work so well.

Recently, I wondered if there was a solution to the problem of the terrorist. Rather than ask my mother, whom I figured would be biased to some extent by her own role in the family, I decided to go above her head and use Arny—as best as I could conjure him from his books—to figure it out. And, at the same time, put my family on the therapy couch.

A common reaction to the black sheep member of the family is to simply talk about him behind his back and tolerate his presence at gatherings. Or, in extreme cases, exile him. The gay brother would probably be happier on his own anyway, away from his fundamentalist Christian family. And if Susie wants to be a musician, she's going to have to get used to sleeping on the street. If you kick the loser out of the family, the family becomes a group of winners again, right? Not according to Arny.

Arny explains that the terrorist in a group is not an individual. The terrorist will usually present itself as a person—your little sister with the attitude problem—but that person is simply acting as a receptacle for a role that can be filled by anyone. In his book *Sitting in the Fire*, Arny put it this way: "Just as no one person or group is the mainstream, so no one person or group is the terrorist. We all find ourselves sometimes in the place of power and other times trying to gain vengeance against the abuses of power."

In a group, a contrasting figure will often emerge, an enactor of its "unacceptable" behavior. If you remove the terrorist, all you do is leave the role open for someone else to fill. "Roles in groups are not fixed, but fluid," writes Arny. "They are filled by different individuals and parties over time, keeping the roles in a constant state of flux." If you kick the "bad" person out of the family, that role becomes vacant, and, who knows, you might be the next to fill it.

That's why Arny's solution to the terrorist problem, unlike that of most powerful governments for most of the last century, is to listen to the terrorist faction and try to understand how its point of view is a necessary one for the mainstream culture to embrace.

If my mother were here helping me to explain this concept, she might ask me, how can we in the mainstream be more like terrorists? I'd respond, Mom, are you crazy, we can't all strap bombs to our chests and blow up the world. Then she'd ask me, why not? Her eyes would be really wide open when she asked that, which is the sign that she's speaking metaphorically again. She wants to blow up the world—in theory. She wants us to be willing to shake apart the structures that exist to see *what's really happening*.

In a modern-day secular society that contains within it a marginalized fundamentalist group, the initial question might be, how can the mainstream bring more "belief" into its core values? Perhaps if the mainstream examined itself to see what it believed on a fundamental level, it would discover that extreme secularity had erased some important things, which if identified and revived, might create a more whole society and solve some of the conflicts with the marginalized. But this is all just hypothesis. The process would have to be done with both groups in the room so that a real dialogue could begin. Obviously, the larger scale the group and the problem, the more difficult and multifaceted the dialogue will become.

My father's initial attempt to "fix" things with Andreya—before the infamous Peace Conference—came in the form of two pairs of bright-red inflatable boxing gloves, a picture of Rocky Balboa emblazoned on each one. The gloves, which he brought home with him one evening after work, were made of that same smelly plastic that beach balls are made of. You blew them up with your own breath and then, as quickly as possible, shoved the plug in before too much air had escaped. Once you'd squeezed your fists inside them, the idea was to start whaling at the member of the family you were having a problem with. Looking back, I realize this was my father's way of incorporating a more raw, nonanalytical form of expression into a family culture where unrestrained expressions of emotion were marginalized.

Of course, my sister refused to ever put them on. There's not much satisfaction in punching someone who is telling you to do it.

The rejection of unmediated anger is something that Arny has often observed from mainstream groups. "Hidden 'mainstream' power," he writes, "lies behind the generally unexpressed assumption that oppressed people must dialogue politely to work out their problems, even though someone who feels oppressed usually does not want to speak gently.

"Today, conflict-resolution schools often deal with social issues in an academic fashion and avoid working with the experience of rage. The mainstream in every country tends to skirt the anger of the oppressed classes. Politics and psychology pressure outsiders to assimilate and integrate. Western thought is biased toward peace and harmony. That's why many non-mainstream groups consider the very idea of 'conflict resolution' a mainstream fabrication.

"Ironically, procedures that implicitly or explicitly forbid anger ultimately provoke conflict, because they favor people who are privileged enough to live in areas where social struggles can be avoided."

I used the gloves, of course, but not really in the way my father intended. My friend Charlie and I spent hours reenacting Mike

Tyson boxing matches and once we got our hands into those gloves, they were quickly filled with too many holes for tape to patch up.

In a way, it's all academic at this point. The political dynamics of my family didn't get a chance to be fully played out because, in the middle of these negotiations and interventions, a more serious revolution was about to take place.

In my memory it's a weekend, but I'm not sure that's accurate. It could have been any afternoon. The structure of my twelve-year-old routine had been dismantled to the point of causing a disorientation of time. The day before, my parents had filed divorce papers. The reasons behind this could fill up a year's worth of analysis, but the salient fact of it at that time was that my mother was leaving my father for another man.

Andreya, my father, and I were out in the front yard talking. The grass hadn't been cut for a few weeks, but we weren't sitting on the grass. We were sitting on our old family room carpet, because the real estate agent who was selling our house said she wouldn't put our house on the market until we replaced the brown shag with something new. I kind of felt like we were all stuck to that carpet, like if we stepped off it we would drown.

Up until that point, I'd just assumed everything was going to continue on as it had, but now I saw that routine was only the stand-in for what really lies beneath. What's *really happening*, as Arny, or my mother, might say. And in this case, my mother *was* saying it.

My father was angry. He was sad. And right then, there was nobody that was going to take that away from him. I don't remember the exact words that he spoke to us out there on the front lawn, but his pain drew me to him. I remember wondering why, in the previous weeks, my mother hadn't simply looked up at the ceiling and described what she saw.

It was weird—the three of us being out there on that island without my mother. My father, my sister, and I had rarely formed any kind of cohesive unit. What was weirder was that not only was I sympathizing with my father, but my sister was as well. She couldn't believe that my mother had gone off with this other guy. She was touching my father's arm sweetly and, I think, mourning the oncoming end of a family in which she had always been the outsider.

It seemed that, momentarily, my sister was no longer the terrorist in our family.

This wouldn't last very long. Only weeks after that afternoon on the lawn, my sister would be headed off to live with my mother in a different city and I'd be off to live with my father. Tensions between my sister and my father would once again rise and result in the near silence that exists between them today. But that time on the island still exists, as a possibility.

I sat there that day silently and witnessed my father and my sister speaking to each other as if they'd always been close.

2

Dreambody

(The Volcano on My Father's Nose)

About a year before my parents' divorce, something started growing on my father's nose, on the side of his left nostril. When it appeared, it looked like a small pimple that would eventually burst and disappear. But then it remained. I worried after a while that it was Lyme disease. I was eleven years old and at that time movie previews included a public service announcement warning people to look out for red spots on their skin that might be Lyme disease, which could kill you. Since red spots were appearing on my own skin all the time, I was in a constant state of thinking I was dying, though my father repeatedly assured me that I was not.

"Then why do I have that red spot?" I'd ask, the leg of my pajama pants pulled up to display said spot on my shin. "And that one."

"I don't know, Micah," my father would say. "But I'm sure it's fine." I pushed, but he never made a guess as to what any of the red spots were that mysteriously appeared on my leg only to disappear and relocate a few days later. I often went to sleep wondering if I was going to wake up the next morning.

But my paranoia about my own red spots was quieted in the face of the thing on my father's nose, which did not move and did not go away. It just slowly, but surely, grew.

I looked through *The ABC's of Nature*, a thick illustrated encyclopedia that my uncle had bought me for Christmas. I had been able to count on this book to explain things to me. It included a section on the human body, which I had visited already several times to view and then review the colorful two-dimensional cross sections of human genitalia. Scientists, it seemed, knew *everything*. I searched for an explanation of the red spots but found nothing. I looked up Lyme disease in the index and was surprised it was not there. "Disease" was listed, but when I went to the page, there wasn't anything resembling what my father had. He really was going to die, I thought.

After a couple weeks, my father finally went to a doctor, who gave him some cream to apply, which was supposed to make it go away. But it didn't work. The alien spot continued to grow. I thought about something a kid at school had once told me, that when bumps on your body get that big, it means that there are spider eggs in it, and that when the eggs are ready to hatch, hundreds of baby spiders come busting through your skin and stream down your face.

One evening, I was leaving my room and saw my father in his own bedroom across the hallway. He was alone, leaning into his

bedside lamp, his face lit up like a patient on an operating table
in the otherwise dark room. He was holding a round vanity mirror, which he shifted from right to left, keeping his eyes forward
on his nose, on the *thing*. In the mirror, he must have seen me
approaching silently from behind.

"What do you think it is, Micah?" he asked, turning his face—
and his Mount Everest—toward me.

"Is it Lyme disease?"

He laughed and turned back to his examination. "I don't think
so," he said. "But it certainly is odd."

In 1987, when the dome on my father's nose appeared, he didn't
have to rely on Western medicine alone to solve his physical ail-
ments. By then he was deeply entrenched in Arny's teachings
about interpreting things that happen to the body as if they are
symbols in a dream. A swelling bump like the one my father had
was actually an exciting happening for him—a chance to listen to
his unconscious.

One morning, while my father and I were eating breakfast, I
asked him if he had any news about his nose. The thing was now
as big as four or five zits stacked on top of each other. (I'd never
had a zit, but my sister had had many, so I knew what they looked
like.)

"I did a process on it," he said.

"And what did the process say?" I asked. At eleven, I was already
fluent in Arny.

"Well, when I imagined into it, I discovered that it was a giant volcano that was threatening to destroy the nearby village and wipe out its entire population." My father spoke enthusiastically, thrilled by what he'd learned from the process. I knew that part of the Jungian and Process Work philosophy was that death in dreams and fantasies usually meant transformation, which was considered a good thing. Still, I worried about all those imaginary people living in the village next to the volcano on my father's nose. *The ABC's of Nature* contained a long section on volcanoes with many photographs. The searing lava that poured from the erupting volcano, the book informed me, destroyed all life in its path. Afterward, when it cooled down, all that was left was the black igneous rock.

In the early 1970s, when Arny was studying quantum physics and psychology and trying to find links between the physical world and the psyche, he was also working with terminally ill patients, some of whom he discovered could not speak. This didn't stop him from working with them though. "[They] initiated me into modes of nonverbal communication whose significance I otherwise would have overlooked," he says.

Arny explains in one of his books that since he was not able to conduct normal talking therapy with many of these patients, he had to rely on other signals: twitches, scratching, unconscious hand movements, coughing tics. "In particular, these patients showed me how to 'amplify' somatic processes, and helped me to define the dreambody," he wrote.

Jung had originally used the term *amplification* to mean taking a client's personal dream figure or symbol and spinning it into a more elaborate story by finding a parallel figure or symbol in mythology and fairy tales. As well as using mythology, Arny's version of amplification asks clients to role play the figure in a dream or imaginatively take a dream story further than the dream itself had provided. But more importantly, he considered his patients' involuntary physical movements as overlooked forms of communication from the unconscious—the same as dreams—and so would ask his clients who couldn't speak to exaggerate these movements, to amplify them. He was trying to get to the bottom of what their body was trying to say, and this "speaking body" is what he meant by the *dreambody*.

As part of his basic philosophy, Arny stopped looking at symptoms—and even more serious conditions like cancer and emphysema—as "illnesses," reasoning that this was too narrow a way to look at what happened to the body. He thought the conception of the body as simply a physical object that is acted upon by diseases and then needs to be repaired was fundamentally flawed. The outdated scientific view, Arny hypothesized, was a holdover from when "molecules and atoms were imagined as baseballs which bounced off walls and obeyed laws of cause and effect." Quantum physics, he argued, proved that bodies large and small were not as fixed and predictable as we once thought. Their physical existence was dependent on the relative position of whatever or whoever was observing them and, in fact, particles could be in two places at the same time. So, he concluded, we also should reevaluate the idea that abnormalities occurred in the physics of our bodies in a cause-and-effect way and, like particles, we might exist in our bodies *and* outside our bodies at the same time.

"In dreams, as in quantum theory, immeasurable yet experiential parts of you are not located only on a street corner or island on the planet Earth," he wrote. "Neither are you located only in this solar system or even in the Milky Way. Rather, you are located in consensus reality on that point of the map, *and* simultaneously in dreamland you are spread throughout the universe. For you to believe that your body is located solely at a particular spot on the planet may disturb your personal relationships and create symptoms as well." In other words, it is not just the cold weather or the fact that you let your friend's toddler sneeze on you that gave you a cold, but the fact that you're too much stuck on this idea that you live on the earth, that your body ends at your fingers and toes.

"Chronic symptoms are *koans*—apparently unanswerable questions meant to increase our consciousness," writes Arny. Doing a "process"—exaggerating and role playing as he'd done with his terminally ill patients at the very beginning—was his method to get to the bottom of what the body was trying to say, and at least reach for the answer.

A process can go many ways, but one example is the time Arny spoke to a finger. Or rather, listened to a finger. Arny was engaged in what he describes in his book *Dreambody* as "a boring conversation" with a client, when he noticed that the client was scratching the arm of his chair with his index finger. At that point, Arny "encouraged the process." He doesn't elaborate on what occurred after that, but from years of observing my parents doing similar things, I have an idea. He'd likely first ask the client to become aware of what he was doing—the scratching. At that point, the client naturally would stop doing it out of self-consciousness. Arny would get the client to start doing it again, but this time to do it *even more*. So the client would start making giant scratching motions, using his whole arm and then body until he transformed into a clawlike Caterpillar backhoe. Arny might then ask the client to speak as if he were the digging machine—"What would the clawlike backhoe machine say?"—or he might have the client act out the excavation on Arny himself, so that Arny could respond and turn the process into a physical dialogue.

In the case of the finger in Arny's book, "Dig! Dig deeper and deeper!" was the client's—I mean, finger's—verbal expression. As it turned out, Arny tells us, the client had recently had a dream whose message had inspired him to be less superficial and more engaged in the "deeper" part of his personality. So it all fit, and once the client was made conscious of this desire to change, Arny says he stopped scratching the upholstery during sessions. He was cured!

My father's Process Work realization that he had a volcano on his nose, however, did not make it go away. And whatever the doctor had given him to apply also wasn't working. So, a week or so after he'd told me about the volcano, he went back to the doctor and had it sliced off. That morning, my father had a volcano on his nose and in the evening he did not. But when he came home that day, he had something else on his face that was even more disturbing—a bandage. It wasn't just a little flesh-colored Band-Aid like the ones I constantly seemed to be wearing on my elbows and knees, but a complicated contraption that captured all your attention when you were speaking to him. My father looked like he'd been through a violent beating.

The wound did heal over, however, and eventually he removed the gauze and tape, uncovering a bright red scab. It looked painful, but the volcano was gone.

Arny warns that you can't stop something that is *trying to happen*. You can forcibly remove a symptom through surgery or drugs, but the underlying reason that it arrived—the thing that it was *trying to say*—could still harm you if it was not listened to and obeyed. My father had de-volcanoed his nose, but in the end, that wasn't going to stop the annihilation of the village. It wasn't going to stop the divorce.

I was sitting with my mother on a lawn of well-maintained grass in the courtyard of a campus in Portland, Oregon. For the previous week, my sister and I had been staying with old friends of my parents' who lived nearby, while my parents attended an Arny workshop. A month had passed since my father's minor nose operation, though the area was still red. I suppose it was good fodder for more processes while they were there, though I don't remember hearing about them and my father wasn't with my mother and me on the lawn that day. My parents had just told my sister and me that my mother was going to stay on in Portland for another few weeks for more Process Work training while my father took us back home. She wanted to spend a little time with me alone before I flew back to Colorado.

"Did you have a good week?" my mother asked me. "Did you play cards a lot?"

I told her a bit about my week staying with her friends, and then I mentioned I'd had a nightmare.

"Oh. Do you want to tell me?"

I told her the dream. It was one of the recurring dreams I had as a child in which I was being chased by something evil. This one was peculiar, however, because the pursuer wasn't a person but an inanimate object.

"It was a stamp, like those hot things they brand cows with," I told her when she asked me to describe it. "It was chasing me and changing shapes."

"Where did the stamp come from, do you think?"

"It was the devil's stamp," I said.

Following some of the things she had learned about Process Work and was in the midst of learning right there in Portland, she asked me if I would act it out.

"How do I do that?" I asked.

"Just pretend to be the stamp, and stamp me."

I nodded. I was a kid, so I was used to pretending to be people and things that I wasn't. I began quickly and violently gnarling my arms out in front of my body, then suddenly froze in a tangled position and pretended to strike my mother as if branding her with the fiery shape of my limbs. I didn't actually touch her but she recoiled, shocked by the intensity. Then I tornadoed my arms again and came at her with another shape. I did this several times until she asked me what the stamp or the devil might say, if it could talk.

I thought about it for a few seconds. "I want to transform you!" I shouted. "I want to hurt you." My mother told me to continue doing the stamp motion, so I did, and she asked me to repeat the words that the stamp would be saying.

Then all of the sudden she was crying. I was surprised because I had rarely seen her cry and when she did cry it never happened because of something I had done. I stopped doing the stamp and she stopped asking me questions about it. I sat quietly and just watched her.

"I'm going to hurt you," she said. "I'm sorry."

But my mother wasn't going to hurt me, I thought. Why would she do that?

"You're not going to hurt me," I said.

"Yes . . . I am." She wiped away her tears.

She didn't elaborate on what she thought she was going to do and I didn't ask. She collected herself, dried her face with a tissue, and hugged me. She told me she loved me. Then we got up and left the lawn.

Although he worked less directly with the body than Arny, Jung was one of the first psychologists to make connections between physiology and the psyche. The anecdotes Jung shares in his memoir have since become typical of Hollywood movies, where the mentally ill person is stuck in an institution and meanwhile he or she is not just nuts but in fact his or her insanity has a meaning, and is even telling a story.

In one case, Jung observed a patient who had been bedridden for forty years and who would make "curious rhythmic motions with her hands and arms." Jung could not explain what the motions were, but after she died, he talked to family members about her personal history and discovered that she had once been a shoemaker desperately in love with another shoemaker. The love was unrequited. When Jung pressed the relatives for a timeline of the woman's deteriorating mental state, he discovered that she'd fallen in love shortly before she went crazy. The strange arm and hand movements were not random after all, Jung realized. All that time, she'd been obsessively making the motions of a street cobbler threading shoes.

Another client of Jung's was a schizophrenic woman who heard voices. She told Jung they "were distributed throughout her entire body, and a voice in the middle of the thorax was 'God's voice.'" Instead of simply writing off these pronouncements as the meaningless symptoms of mental illness as most doctors of the time would have, Jung told her to listen to the voice in her thorax. "We must rely on that voice," he told her. When encouraged, the voice insisted that Jung test the woman on the Bible. Jung decided to go with it. Each time he visited, he assigned her pages of the Bible to read and during the following visit quizzed her. After six years, she told him that the voices no longer possessed her whole body and were now only present in the left half. "Hence it must be concluded," he wrote, "that the patient was cured—at least halfway."

In his memoir, Jung also shares a personal story about an illness caused by family conflict from when he was about three years old. "I am restive, feverish, unable to sleep," he remembers. "My father carries me in his arms, paces up and down, singing his old student songs . . . I was suffering, so my mother told me afterward, from general eczema. Dim intimations of trouble in my parents' marriage hovered around me. My illness, in 1878, must have been connected with a temporary separation of my parents. My mother spent several months in a hospital in Basel, and presumably her illness had something to do with the difficulty in the marriage."

The memory is strikingly similar to one of my own. When I was growing up, whenever my parents fought, they reassured me that it was okay, they were not going to break up—they were going to be together "forever." Even at a young age, I didn't really buy it, since I already had evidence that their relationship was not infallible.

Before I was even a year old, my father had doubts about settling down into family life and he'd also met another woman. He decided to give the new relationship a chance, so my mother took my sister and me and moved from Wyoming to Denver. At the time, my mother was working as a secretary, barely making ends meet. The stress of caring for two kids was too much for her. After a few months, she called my father and told him he had to take me. He did and then about six months later, I came down with a case of diarrhea so severe that my father took me to the hospital. He called my mother to let her know. She returned with Andreya to Wyoming to visit me and, as the scene would appear in the movie version of real events, she and my father gazed through the glass window at me, their baby, sleeping on a miniature hospital bed, then slowly turned their heads toward each other so that their eyes met, and in those eyes they saw a love that would save their marriage—well, for another twelve years. This was the story they told me and so I always considered my illness as a kind of dreambody intervention on my part that had kept the family together.

Except for the six-month lapse when my mother handed me over to my father, she was the one who took care of me when I was sick. If I had, for instance, fallen down and cut my leg, my father would tell me he was sorry I was hurt and offer a Band-Aid. But I wanted someone who would be as upset as I was about the pain and that was my mother.

The worst afflictions happened in my ears—the part of me that my dreambody decided to communicate through incessantly. The infections would start with a feeling of fullness inside the ear canal and soon I couldn't hear so well. Then the burning would begin and it would become relentless. I couldn't think, couldn't do anything but moan and cry. My mother would hold me in her arms and stroke my hair as I ground my teeth and tensed all my muscles in agony. She would tell me it was going to be alright. After a while, she'd take me to the bathroom, lean my head over the bathtub, and pour warmed oil into my ear. I don't remember whether the oil eased any of the pain, but the rituals of her caretaking calmed me.

The infections continued past childhood, when most people stop having them, and by the time I was a teenager I was diagnosed with a chronic condition that my doctor treated by inserting tiny plastic tubes in my eardrums. To my initial relief, the tubes—which helped air flow into the inner ear—ended the infections. But whenever the tubes fell out, as they were designed to do eventually, the infections would start again where they'd left off. The first infection after a tube fell out was always a depressing moment and I'd go to my mother for comforting. I remember one particular time especially because it happened at work when I was in my early twenties.

"Hi, Mom," I whispered into the phone, my tie snaked into a pile on my desk as I bent out of sight in my cubicle, covering my mouth and the receiver with my hand.

"I'm okay," I said when she asked me in a concerned voice if everything was alright, "but my ear is starting to hurt."

"Oh no," she said in her sympathetic mom voice. "Well, when you think about the pain, is there a picture in your head?" It was embarrassing to be doing this at work, but it was why I had called. Having these discussions with my mother had become soothing in the way the heated oil used to be.

"A balloon," I said. "A pink balloon."

"A pink balloon," she repeated, then paused. "What would it feel like to be a pink balloon?"

We then got into a prolonged discussion in which I described the attributes of being a pink balloon. To be a pink balloon meant being light, meant being spontaneous, of course. It meant laughing and smiling, flying high! My mother got excited when I described the balloon to her and in her soothing voice she encouraged me to try and live my life like a pink balloon.

I always wanted it to work. I wanted this new way of living—the pink balloon way of living—to solve the problems with my ears. I sometimes thought if I followed her directions, the whole condition with my ear would magically just disappear. But it always came back.

Whenever I'd be at the doctor's having a new incision cut into my eardrum and new tubes put in, I could hear Arny, speaking as if perched on the shoulder of my good ear: You can't stop what's *trying to happen*. I'd wave him away and let the doctor operate. Eventually, the repeated surgeries and tubes caused a permanent tear in my right eardrum, significantly impairing hearing.

Over the years, my friends more than once have accused me of getting sick too often.

How can you get sick *too* often, I'd ask them. You're either sick or you're not sick. But whenever I'd say I was not feeling up to coming out for drinks, they'd repeat this judgment, often adding that it was "all in my head."

One night after I'd suffered their collective noncompassion during a winter break visit home from university, I went into the bathroom and looked at myself in the mirror.

"I'm not sick," I said. I waited for a good feeling to wash over me. It did not. My ear was starting to hurt a little and I thought it was probably infected. I opened the cabinet to find a bottle of liquid antibiotics. The doctor had said I should keep some

on hand in case I ever had pain. I knew this was shoddy medical practice, but after all the ear infections I'd had in my life,
I'd gotten somewhat lazy. The doctor always just gave me more
antibiotics anyway. When I saw that there were more than a few
of those bottles collecting dust in the cabinet, I thought maybe
my friends were right—I did get sick a lot. So maybe it *was* something that was just in my head, I thought, but what was I supposed to do about it? Even if I accepted that to be true, that
hardly made things any easier. How does one "fix" one's head?
I shook my head in the mirror and my reflection shook its head
back at me. If I could simply change my mind about things and
that would actually make a difference, I'd always be healthy, I'd
be a millionaire, and I'd have a really hot girlfriend. I took off my
shirt and for fun tried for a minute to will myself defined pectoral
muscles. Then I tilted my head, turned my ear up and put three
drops into it, waiting as the cold liquid slid its way down into my
ear canal.

"See life as a disease *you* have chosen and then you will remember who you are." When I read that sentence in Arny's *Dreambody,*
I thought it economically summed up his philosophy of how to
look at illness. The sentence is preceded by Arny's discussion of
a folk tale in which the god Mercury is asked by a woodsman to
prove his greatness by squeezing himself into a little bottle. He
does so, and after the woodsman traps him in there, Mercury must
promise favors to his captor to get back out. Mercury, Arny says,
symbolizes our true life energy, our spirit, which wants to be free.
And like this myth, he suggests, modern people were constantly

constraining themselves, bottling up their feelings. In our day-to-day life, this means choosing stable careers and setting long-term goals despite what we really want to be doing in the moment. Our bodies suffer, Arny asserts, because we give ourselves diseases to push us to wake us up and live our true dreams.

While they've both now moved on from Process Work in their own ways, for much of the time I was growing up my parents encouraged me to think about what a symptom was doing to me, how I could turn things around and be the doer instead of the done to, how I could become the pink balloon instead of the pink balloon infecting me.

I like the idea in principle, but there's always been one sticking point for me: It would be way easier to just continue feeling sorry for myself.

In one of his books, Arny gives a specific example of how Process Work helped one of his clients, a man who had emphysema. When Arny asked this client to act out his earliest memory, the activity leads the man to describe his mother as "always bitter and cramped." As Arny talked him through this further, the man realized that all his life, he'd been compensating for his mother's cold disposition by being overly nice and concerned with other people. Arny suggested he should stop trying to correct his mother's ways in his own life and at the end of the session Arny says the man had "found a sort of cool detachment and freedom from always being too nice to people, and he was much happier." Not long after that, the client's emphysema symptoms disappeared completely.

I understand from stories like this that if I own up to the fact that I am the one torturing my ears, if I figure out what I am overcompensating for, my eardrum will be restored! But I'm unwilling so far to take the blame. I feel guilty about not actively healing myself in this way. Sometimes, the guilt of not taking the blame and thus allowing—or causing—my ears to get worse and worse produces so much anxiety in me that I have found myself sitting on the couch motionless in a sweat worrying that at any moment my other eardrum will collapse and I'll go deaf.

In fact, the dreambody philosophy has been so ingrained in me that at times in my life, I came into contact with something that would probably be better described as *paranoidbody*. It went like this: I made advance plans to go out Friday night. On Friday, I'm feeling kind of down and don't really want to see anyone. But I have to keep the commitment, I think to myself. Then I remember the dreambody. I remember that if I don't follow these gut instincts coming from my unconscious, I will get sick. I start to notice that my nose seems a little stuffed up. And my ears, are they starting to fill up with fluid? It's hard to tell, but maybe. In fact, I might already be doomed to become ill simply because I haven't canceled already! But wait, this is all nonsense. A little decision of going out for a drink when I don't absolutely want to can't really make me sick. Arny didn't intend for me to take it this far, did he? I'm sure he could straighten it out for me if he were here. But get a grip on yourself. Forget Arny. If I go out, I'll probably cheer up and be in a good mood and I won't get sick at all. I'll just have a hangover tomorrow. And it goes on like this until my mind collapses and I just make a decision.

Maybe my friends are right. It is all in my head. All in my crazy, hypochondriac head.

When my father, my sister, and I arrived back home from the Arny seminar in Portland, things were odd with my mother gone. Although she was a small, quiet person, it became clear that she was the primary disciplinarian. Without her there, my sister and I were able to persuade my father to let us have more dessert and then get away with not brushing our teeth before going to bed. The Saturday after we returned, my father brought us to his office to record a videotape to send to my mother, to remind her of her family back home.

My father had a video camera in his office for the purpose of taping therapy sessions so that he could watch them later and, like a football coach viewing last week's game, go over which psychological "plays" had worked best. On the tape we made for my mother, my father is smiling a lot like he does in photos, which looks different from his actual smile when he's happy or laughing at a joke. It's a smile, but one that has a frown hovering at its edges, an obvious overcompensation for his uneasiness. If I were his Process Work therapist, I would recommend he frown *even more* and see what that felt like. Maybe the frowning dad would have something to say that would be a truer expression of his feelings.

I spend most of the time in the video running circles around Andreya and doing cartwheels. This is my obvious attempt to lighten the situation. Being a sensitive boy, I could tell my father was sad, so I was trying to be as distracting and hilarious as possible. My sister was for once collaborating with my father, answering some questions about her life monosyllabically. She smiled and waved to my mother. The analysis of Andreya's behavior was more straightforward: She missed her mother.

When my mother returned, everything went back to normal for a month. And then one night, unraveled.

Dinner had ended a long time ago. I was in the living room next to the kitchen playing with blocks, setting up soldiers on fortifications I'd built. Meanwhile, a giant robot was making its way over from the opposite side of the room to come and crush them. My mother was sitting at the dinner table with my father and sister, talking about something serious. The voices in the kitchen were muffled, but I'd managed to make out that my parents' best friends were thinking about getting a divorce. It was sad news because their children had also been close friends of my sister's and mine since we were little. I decided to stay in the living room because there was a lot of warfare to get through by bedtime.

Then, all of a sudden, my father started making a groaning noise like a dog run over in the road. I was called in. I told them I was busy and didn't want to come—the robot was just arriving at the fort—but they insisted.

When I walked in, my sister was crying, which was not unusual. She cried often, sometimes while watching the evening news.

"I met someone else," my mother said when I sat down. For some reason my father was sitting in my chair, so I'd had to take his spot next to her.

I stared at the chipped wood of the table as my father became emotional and started shouting. I wasn't listening to the words, but when he paused and began crying I looked up at him. His face was red, the blood vessels at his temples raised and pulsing.

He caught his breath. "I feel like a nuclear bomb just exploded on my life," he said. I saw a mushroom cloud rising into the sky above our suburb, the explosion vaporizing our house and all the houses surrounding ours. That thing on my father's nose, healed at that point, kind of did look like the site of nuclear aftermath, pale white and flat. My sister started crying even harder, the most she'd cried since Reagan had gone on television to say that we were close to war with the Russians. Back then, she'd bled all over the place because she'd had a tooth pulled earlier in the day.

There was hope, my mother assured us. "There's just a 5 percent chance that this other thing will happen," she said.

I figured quickly this meant that there was a 95 percent chance that everything would work out okay and remain the same. But I knew—I suppose children have an intuition about these things— that the 5 percent was a superpowerful 5 percent. That 5 percent was like the robot against the soldiers. It was just one robot, but it stood high above them. Their puny weapons could not puncture its armor. The robot would win.

My father must have felt the same way because he didn't seem reassured. The conversation went on for a while longer and once again I stopped listening. I stared at the wood of the table again and then at my sister and mother, thinking about how this is what my father sees when we're eating dinner. Eventually, my mother couldn't take being there any longer and she went over and sat on the stairs that went down to the family room. She put her head in her hands and told us that she wished she'd never been born.

I was standing above her when she said that, and I wanted to comfort her, but I didn't know what to say. If my mother had never been born, then what about me?

It was a warm summer night, a pleasant night for a walk. After my mother had collected herself, there was a feeling that the worst was over and maybe we'd get through it alive. My father suggested we take a walk to the convenience store to get ice cream. Where we lived, the nearest store was a twenty-minute walk away. It was late and nobody was in the streets—just the four of us walking like a pack of apocalypse survivors over the old, gray streets. The concrete was worn away in many places so that you could see the stones and pebbles the road was made of. I could feel them through the soles of my shoes.

Oddly, I was happy. My sister had taken me under her wing, talking with me more intimately than ever before and cracking jokes to make me laugh. Perhaps because we'd been to the brink but were still together, I felt closer to my family than I ever had. When we got to the store, Andreya saw that they served root beer floats and asked my parents if we could get one. They said yes, we could get whatever we wanted.

The weeks after the night my mother dropped the bomb were odd to say the least. The usual strangeness that Jungian and Arny-inspired practices introduced into the house reached a fever pitch. Arny might say that the dreambody comes out most in times of crisis, but as a child I interpreted the prevalence of Process Work in my house as a desperate attempt by my father to save his marriage. Once I realized that the emotional catharsis of the root beer float night wasn't going to be enough, I stopped being happy. I worried.

At one point, my father had taken to speaking as if he were Daffy Duck. I understood even back then that this was presumably done as a result of my father's exaggerating some body impulse he'd had. It could be comical, a grown man squelching all of his words so as to sound ducklike. My father had often made me laugh by changing his voice or taking on some made up accent for one of my stuffed animals. But at the time, I wished more than anything that everyone would just go back to normal.

On my twelfth birthday, my father finally became the volcano. My parents were having an argument, which led to my father abruptly packing his clothes. But instead of pulling out the drawers of his dresser one by one and removing the articles of clothing to place them on the bed and then into a suitcase, he was tearing each drawer out and, from what I could hear, hurling them across their bedroom.

My father's eruption frightened me because I'd never witnessed such violence from him before. In my room, I crouched into a ball, with my knees folded under me, my head down, and my hands over my ears. I decided that nothing was going to touch me inside of that ball.

My father never finished packing. He left the house and got into his Jeep and drove off. I worried that he was going to drive his truck over a cliff and I wished that someone would go after him. In my ball, I prayed that he would come back home safe.

———————

I don't blame my father for becoming the volcano. He owned the violence of his emotions and I think that's what saved him from being a crushed villager. That may not have been the case for me, however.

Several years later, in high school, I was hanging out with my friend Jacob in my room. He asked me why the bottom drawer of my dresser, which had been passed down to me from my father, was falling apart. I told him the volcano story and even reenacted how I'd crouched down into the ball.

"Maybe you should do a process on that," he said. Jacob had picked up Process Work thirdhand, but he was a quick learner.

"Sure, why not," I said, waiting for him to ask me a question. He stared at me for a few moments before I remembered that he wasn't a psychologist so had no idea what he was supposed to do.

I got down on the floor and crouched into the ball.

"So I'm supposed to say what I feel like," I told Jacob.

"Okay," he said. "So? What do you feel like?"

"I'm a stone," I said.

"You're stoned?" Jacob laughed, because in fact we were.

"No, I'm a stone!"

"Okay, okay. So, you're a stone. Okay."

"Hmm, but not just a stone. I'm also an egg."

"An egg and a stone?"

"Yes, I am the stone egg man," I declared.

"Coo coo ca choo," he replied.

That weekend, Jacob and I got high and headed to the mountains. We were browsing through a tourist knickknack store and I was mesmerized by a rainbow-colored whirligig when Jacob appeared suddenly before me with a look of awe in his eye. "Look at this," he said, dramatically holding forth a small black object in his hand. "A stone egg."

Finally, when it became clear that the 95 percent chance my parents were going to stay together wasn't going to happen, my father moved to the city and got himself a small basement apartment. It was decided that I would stay in our house with my mother until I finished sixth grade. In the meantime, I'd visit my father every other weekend. But I was angry that I could not see my father every day. When I learned his new phone number, I repeated it over and over again in my head, memorizing it.

Then one night, I took a ballpoint pen and violently carved the number into the top of my dresser.

Shortly after he moved out, my mother had a dream where rain was pouring down for days and wouldn't stop. It was raining so much that all the land was flooding. When she woke up from the dream, she couldn't figure out what it was about. But then the next night, as she was putting me to bed, I asked her if she would get into my bed with me and hold me. She hesitated for a moment, her Freudian taboo instinct worrying momentarily that I was trying to take my place as the new man of the house, but she decided it was okay. She laid herself down and put her arms around me.

"What's wrong?" she said. I was crying.

"I want to go live with Dad," I told her.

3

The Oedipus Complex

(My Mother's Small Lover)

For many a man hath seen himself in dreams
His mother's mate, but he who gives no heed
To such like matters bears the easier fate.
—Sophocles, *Oedipus Tyrannus*

When I masturbated, which at fifteen years old I did twice daily, I thought of various things. Michelle, the girl in my grade whom I'd had a crush on since the beginning of freshman year, made regular appearances. Sometimes—I suppose because I thought there was no chance in hell she would ever go out with me—we were both naked and strapped down to rectangular metal tables, slowly pressed into each other by captor sex scientists. Another common theme was the topless woman in white underwear whose picture I kept under my bed, a Calvin Klein advertisement I'd ripped out of a magazine. I didn't have to look at it anymore because as far as images of half-naked women were concerned, I had what people call a photographic memory. If I was feeling energetic, I'd run around my room pretending that I was a soldier, shooting and getting shot at. Eventually, I'd get tagged by machine gun fire. (I threw a glass of water on myself to simulate a blood-soaked shirt.) I'd be rescued by a helicopter and brought to the field hospital, where I was taken care of by a nurse. A hot nurse. A hot nurse who would hike up her uniform, have sex with me, and then bring other hot nurses around to also have sex with me. And then there was my mother.

Wait a minute! My mother?

And that's how it happened—totally out of the blue. I was going along fantasizing about the nurses, and then—*blam!*—there was my mother. I pulled my hand away from myself and lay there paralyzed for a minute, utterly confused, my heart pounding both from the shock and also from the act I'd been engaged in, which I now didn't want to think about at all. What was my mother doing popping into my head while I was getting myself off? I started repressing the thought immediately—Freud would be proud—but that damned photographic memory turned against me and all I could see after that was my mother's face, her smiling eyes framed with her short brown hair and dangly aquamarine earrings. I went limp—thank you, my dear dreambody, for that—and abandoned the whole procedure for the night. But this was no small thing to recover from. The next day, I was as chaste as a monk. I didn't touch myself at all, breaking a world record–bound streak that went back at least three years. But I knew even then that celibacy wasn't a permanent solution. I could not give up my favorite pastime. I was caught between the vision of my mother and a hard place.

Thankfully, after that, my mother never made another surprise appearance—well, except in person once when she entered my room without knocking while I was busy with myself under the sheets, something she didn't notice or else we both pretended wasn't happening. The mind has a way of wandering during masturbation, sometimes even to mundane tasks or what one ate for lunch. I might have even forgotten all about the "unfortunate vision"—as a friend of mine once called it—if it weren't for the fact that my parents are psychologists and Freud, along with Jung, was commonly brought up around the dinner table. Every once in a while over the years, I've remembered my mother's cameo and have wondered why it might have happened.

Freud, our dear founder of psychoanalysis, might say it started with the nurses. Not the hot nurses from my fantasies, but the evil ones who took me away from my mother just after she gave birth to me. My mother had explicitly told them that I was not to be bottle-fed, because she'd heard that sometimes infants would then refuse to breast-feed, and she wanted to breast-feed me. Her request, however, got lost in the postbirth shuffle and I ended up being given a bottle, after which I did in fact refuse to breast-feed for quite some time. It chokes me up to think about my refusing my mother's milk. "I didn't mean it!" I wish to call out to her now across the hundreds of miles that separate us.

According to Freud, baby Micah initially missed out on one of the key Oedipal moments. Freud says that our mothers are our first love-objects and, as such, breastfeeding is the original consummation. "At the time at which the first beginnings of sexual satisfaction are still linked with the taking of nourishment," Freud wrote, "the sexual instinct has a sexual object outside the infant's own body in the shape of the mother's breast." For baby Micah, the difficulty of attaining this "sexual satisfaction" might have caused him some baby-scaled separation anxiety, which he was simply overcompensating for later as a teenager. Of course, this would be taking Freud literally, something one should rarely do.

Freud was already developing psychoanalysis—with its emphasis on the long-lasting traumas of early sexuality—when he came across Sophocles' play *Oedipus Tyrranus*, which he synopsizes as the story of a man "who was destined by fate to kill his father and take his mother to wife."

Freud read the play over two thousand years after it was first performed and he felt he could explain why it had such lasting power. He believed its psychological strength was not simply due to it being a well-written tragedy by an accomplished playwright or that it broaches the compelling question of who is ultimately responsible for morally reprehensible acts—the gods or men. "It is not to [morality] that the auditor reacts but to the secret sense and content of the legend," Freud wrote. "He reacts as though by self-analysis he had recognized the Oedipus complex in himself and had unveiled the will of the gods and the oracle as exalted disguises of his own unconscious." In other words, like Oedipus, as young boys—as toddlers, even—we want to sleep with our mothers. Overcoming this desire is a normal part of growing up, but when we view Sophocles' ancient tale of a man carrying out what we so narrowly escaped, we are horrified by the traces that desire left in our memories.

My parents always frowned on Freud, telling me that he looked into the past to look for pathology while Jung—the good guy in their view—instead focused on the present and future, choosing to see our lives as a process of unfolding toward wholeness. Jung eventually decided Freud had taken this mother-love business way too far, but as a rising star of psychology, Jung publicly supported Freud's theories even if from the beginning, in private correspondence, he expressed some doubts.

In his first letter to Freud, written in 1906 when Jung was thirty-one and Freud fifty, he tells Freud that although he finds his colleague's theory about the cause of mental disorder helpful and the best on offer, he's concerned with its narrow focus. "[I]t seems to me that though the genesis of hysteria is predominantly, it is not exclusively, sexual," Jung wrote. Freud's response was even-handed, but subtly obstinate. "Your writings have long led me to suspect that your appreciation of my psychology does not extend to all my views on hysteria and the problem of sexuality but I venture to hope that in the course of the years you will come much closer to me than you now think possible."

This disagreement was the seed of their eventual break up, though it would be a long six years until that split finally occurred.

One of Jung's consistently expressed frustrations with Freud's sex theory was that in its language it equated the drives of children with those of adults. Freud referred to a child's attachment to his mother as "incestual," and upon reading through some of Freud's books, I was shocked—and amused—at some of his descriptions. "Well, it is easy to see that the little man wants to have his mother all to himself," writes Freud. This reference to a boy as a miniature adult is disconcerting, but in another example, Freud takes it to a cringe-worthy level. In the context of discussing how a daughter's hope to be her father's wife is crushed when he first punishes her and how a son is disappointed to see his mother's affections turn away from him after a sibling is born, Freud writes: "Even when no special events occur, like those we have mentioned as examples, the absence of the satisfaction hoped for, the continued denial of the desired baby, must in the end lead the small lover to turn away from his hopeless longing."

Perhaps the phrase "small lover" comes across differently—and less ridiculously—in German, but somehow I doubt it.

For a while as a teenager, I used to think back to my childhood before the divorce and didn't remember my mother being around much. She was a quiet and introverted person, but it was odd how invisible she seemed. I remembered her frustration when I'd wake her in the middle of the night because I'd peed in my bed. And I remembered her sitting at the piano every night before dinner playing Beethoven. She played the same song over and over again, making five notes of progress a night. It would always start out so beautifully and then slowly come apart, the notes dispersing like marbles falling from her hands until she would stop and start over again. I would sit with my toys and listen to her play, concentrating all my psychic energy on encouraging her to make it to the end, though she never did. A few more things remained as well, but it was almost like she had been erased from my memory.

"I didn't know how to be with kids," my mother told me later as an explanation of why she didn't engage much with me until I was thirteen and more adultlike.

That lack of connection is probably part of why I don't remember her presence, but I've come to think the real reason is because our relationship changed so much after the divorce and in such a short period of time that the mother I knew later—who did engage with me, quite intensely, whom I sometimes thought of more as a friend than a parent—isn't recognizable in the past because she simply didn't exist then.

You'd probably get a different explanation from Freud. He'd say I went through a dysfunctional "latency period." See, you're the small, perhaps jilted lover only until you're about five. Once you figure out that your pudgy hands and your ill-formed uppercut are not going to dethrone your father—and in fact, such aggression might just lead to your castration (look what happened to your sister!)—you become "autoerotic." The case histories are quite varied as to how this plays out, but it could be anything from fondling your willy—my preference—to pressing your bum into the ground to prevent your poo from escaping, because it feels good to have it in there (one of Jung's first letters to Freud detailed such a case).

But, when you're a preteen, you come out of latency and you start seeking a love-object that is not yourself or your excrement. Your mother is still around and she was your first love, so it's natural to consider her again. But your father still seems to be claiming her as his own, and no other kids are making it with their mothers. In fact, you've learned from movies and gossip that this is highly forbidden. You move on, looking for a substitute. Or, as Freud puts it, "The finding of an object is in fact the re-finding of it."

For me, it went a little differently. When I was twelve and starting to form my first serious crushes on girls at school, my parents
divorced and I moved to the city with my father. It was a very
lonely period and I spent a lot of time by myself. My only contact
with my mother was twice-monthly visits. Every other weekend,
I'd head over to her place in Boulder, half an hour from where I
lived with my father in Denver. We only had four days a month
together, but those four days were concentrated bonding time.
My sister had moved out to live with her boyfriend, so my mother
and I spent those four days and nights almost exclusively just the
two of us, without distractions, going out for dinner, seeing films,
taking walks.

"You mean you went on dates," a friend said recently when I
explained how this happened.

"Well, not exactly!" I protested.

But okay, we sort of went on dates.

At thirteen, my mother and I had become equals in height
(she's not a tall woman and I was in the middle of my growth
spurt). While on a weekend visit about six months after I'd moved
in with my father, my mother took me out to the woods for
a hike.

It was a cloud-covered day, had rained earlier, and the path was
wet. The air smelled like pine mixed with something I couldn't
quite put my finger on. Something foul, though.

"It smells like pee," I decided finally.

My mother laughed. "That's the smell of the forest's natural
decay," she said.

We were silent for a while as we hiked. There was no one else out on the path.

"So how are things?" my mother asked me as we rounded the side of the mountain.

"Fine," I said, though it was not true. I'd started seventh grade in a new school, was having a hard time making friends, and was basically miserable.

"Is there anything wrong?"

"No, nothing's wrong." We walked in silence for a minute.

"It's so beautiful out here," she said. I was staring at the ground but looked up to see a sharp drop ahead. It would be easier just to jump, I thought to my angst-ridden melodramatic self.

"Mom, it's just . . . I don't have any friends," I said. "I don't know how to make them."

She put her hand on my shoulder. "I'm sorry to hear that, Micah, but that's not going to be a problem for you. You're so interesting and smart. Just be yourself, and you'll make friends."

"I don't know," I said, but it was nice to be reassured.

I told her about my other problems, which included my battles with my father over chores, my lack of fashion sense, and my fear of talking to girls. She engaged me on these topics without just blowing them off or coming up with clichéd advice. Once the door was open, things just started flooding out and I told her everything.

After our hike, we went shopping for dinner and when I jokingly put a pie in our basket, she said sure, let's have pie. It seemed like something she wouldn't have allowed before. Suddenly, it felt like there were no rules—we could do whatever we wanted. When we returned home, we played a card game that we picked out randomly from a book. Nobody else knew the game or its rules. It was *our* game.

On Sundays, she would take me to the swimming pool and then in the afternoon sit with me to watch the football game, even though she had no idea what all those players were doing out there. All this time, I was falling in love with my mother.

One day, we were looking through old pictures of her family and I came across one of my mother as a thirteen-year-old girl, leaning against the railing of a ship with the Statue of Liberty blurry in the background. At that time, in the early sixties, her family came to America from Germany. It was not the first time they'd come; they'd immigrated to the United States and Canada a few times before but, homesick, had each time returned to Germany. This photograph was from the last trip over, after which they finally stayed put.

My mother told me that the trip across the Atlantic took two weeks, and that during the voyage when the photograph was taken, she had a prolonged flirtation with a twenty-one-year-old man on the ship. She told him that she was older and he believed her, or at least pretended to. They clandestinely followed each other around, hiding in corners to talk, but when they were finally in a room and he tried to make out with her, she ran away. Her parents were completely oblivious to the whole thing.

Freud says that kids come up with elaborate fantasies to enact incestuous desires. Commonly, a boy will fantasize about his father going away on a business trip and never coming back. Or if the incest fantasy involves a sibling, the child will imagine that he is actually the child of other parents—extremely rich, of course—but that he was never told this and so his sister isn't really his sister and he can marry her.

I wondered when I looked at the photograph of my mother as a young girl what it would have been like if I could have met her on that ship. She could have been my girlfriend. And this would not have been incest, because I—the I that is her son—was not yet born. It would be me still, but not the me that was that girl's future son. I wasn't thinking about sex—sorry, Freud—but I wanted somebody to go on adventures with, someone with whom I could share my deepest thoughts and feelings. I couldn't think of anyone more suited to this than my mother, because that's what we were already doing.

Although my father had been removed from the equation, I was not without a rival for my mother's attention. There was Peter, the man my mother had left my father for. However, the two of us didn't end up really rivaling much. My mother introduced me to Peter in the same house my father no longer lived in. He towered over me at six-foot-one and yet approached with the humility of someone genuinely concerned with the emotions of a twelve-year-old boy and his role in them. I quickly adopted him as a second father. Peter was intelligent, funny, and liked listening to my stories. As a somewhat self-righteous teenager, I had as many strong opinions about things as he did. At least one night during my weekends in Boulder, we'd all do dinner and a movie. It was a pleasing intellectual threesome.

One weekend, my mother and "my Peter" took me to see *The Man in the Moon*, a film about a young teenage girl in love with an older boy. The girl was Reese Witherspoon at roughly my age then. I thought she was very beautiful and I wanted her to be in love with me. I ached for this in my angst-ridden teenage heart. The more I thought about it, the more I decided I would probably never fall in love and would be lonely for my entire life until I died.

Back at home, my mother, Peter, and I sat around the kitchen table eating pie and ice cream. As we engaged in a postmortem discussion about the film, my mother asked me if there were any girls I was interested in at school.

"No," I said. I was silent for a few moments, eating my pie, wondering if I could tell her what I was thinking. The two of them were always so open and understanding, I decided I could.

"But I know what kind of person I'd want to go out with," I said.

"What kind?"

"Someone like you."

She smiled. I awkwardly glanced at Peter.

"That's the highest compliment a boy can pay to his mother," he said, and shared that he'd once felt the same way about his mother. I had always thought there was something wrong with this sentiment—the force of the Freudian taboo is strong—so it was nice to hear Peter say that.

"Well, when I was your age, I would have liked to have met someone like you," my mother said.

As I progressed into teenagehood, the frank discussions I had with my mother became an increasingly important part of our relationship. Then, one day when I was seventeen, we talked about sex.

It was a Saturday morning and we were out for brunch as we always were on the Saturdays we were together. I was less conversational than usual, anxious about something that had happened. It was all I could think about, but I wasn't sure if I could really tell anyone else about it. But finally, I decided I could tell my mother.

"Mom," I said in as quiet a voice as I could, "I tried to have sex and I couldn't do it."

"What do you mean?" she asked. She looked concerned.

"I mean . . ." I scanned the tables nearby. "I mean I couldn't get an erection."

"You couldn't get an erection?" she repeated, at full volume.

"Mom!" A couple nearby glanced at us.

"Sorry," she said quietly. She laughed. "I was worried it was something really bad."

"This *is* really bad. What if I can never have sex?" I said, imagining all the celibate years ahead of me from that day until my death, all the gorgeous women just out of my frustrated reach. Life was not worth living anymore. My mother stopped smiling.

"Well," she said, "there is a solution." She nodded silently for a moment, as if verifying to herself that, yes, she knew exactly what to do.

She placed her hands on the table between us.

"You have to *be* the erect penis in your life."

. . .

One of the cornerstones of Jungian psychology is Active Imagination. Some kids are told they have an active imagination, or even an *overactive* imagination, and what is meant by those compliments (or accusations) is pretty much in line with Jung's concept. Practicing Jung's version—another predecessor to Arny's techniques—means deliberately exploring one's imagination and fantasies by creating art projects based on them, or acting them out verbally or physically to read the message that one's unconscious is trying to communicate.

In late 1913, Jung was on a train, traveling alone and daydreaming when he suddenly had a disturbing vision. He saw very clearly in his head the Alps flooded and the mountains around Switzerland rising higher to protect his country from some unknown catastrophe. "I saw the mighty yellow waves, the floating rubble of civilization, and the drowned bodies of uncounted thousands," Jung wrote in his memoir. "Then the whole sea turned to blood."

A couple weeks later, Jung heard what he described as an inner voice that told him to heed these visionary warnings because "it is wholly real and it will be so." Still thinking along Freudian lines at this point, Jung tried to figure out what was wrong with him that made him see these things—what was he repressing? He decided in the end that he was "menaced by a psychosis," though he could not name it.

The next year, the visions turned to dreams where an icy frost descended upon Europe in the middle of summer, killing all living things. And then, that August, the world war broke out. Mystery solved!

Jung realized that he'd tapped into the psyche of "mankind in general," something he would later dub the *collective unconscious*. For the sake of the entire world, Jung felt it was his duty to get to the bottom of his fantasies, so he started developing and practicing what would become Active Imagination. He let the visions overtake him, spoke back to them, embodied characters from them, wrote them down and meditated on them.

"Sometimes it was as if I was hearing it with my ears, sometimes feeling it with my mouth, as if my tongue were formulating words; now and then I heard myself whispering aloud," Jung wrote. "Below the threshold of consciousness everything was seething with life."

From the outside during this time, Jung must have looked a bit nuts, or like a man in a particularly unique midlife crisis. He was not unaware of this fact, and as a scientist, it bothered him. He would much rather have been seeing clients and analyzing clinical data, but alas, he felt compelled to delve into the brave new world of his unconscious. "I was afraid of losing command of myself and becoming a prey to the fantasies—and as a psychiatrist I realized only too well what that meant," he wrote. "After prolonged hesitation, however, I saw that there was no other way out. I had to take the chance, had to try to gain power over them; for I realized that if I did not do so, I ran the risk of their gaining power over me."

The lives of millions were not at stake in my successfully getting it up, but in my teenage assessment of world problems, permanent impotence was only slightly behind mass genocide. I was desperate, would have tried anything, so when my mother asked me if I wanted to do an exercise where I was to "become the erection," I agreed to do it.

"But not here," I said.

My mother drove us to the park where we often started our walks up into the foothills. As we strolled around, looking for a good spot, we passed a couple lying on a blanket making out, stroking each other's hair. I imagined they did the deed two, maybe three, times daily. Then, loping toward us was a balding, middle-aged man, socks yanked up to his knees, three kids in tow. Obviously, his reproductive powers weren't failing. And as I looked around, I became achingly aware that the park, indeed the whole surrounding neighborhood, was peopled with nonvirgins, sexually thriving individuals, no matter how unfashionable or malformed they were.

"So, first we need the question."

"Mom, I think we've covered that already."

"I know, but it helps if we can verbalize it as a question. How about this: How can I act like an erection in my everyday life? Go ahead, ask." I obeyed, mumbling the question.

"Now, listen to your unconscious. Hear what it says, and follow whatever cues it gives you."

I stared at the grass for a few seconds, then, as a joke, began gesturing my fingers wildly out of the top of my head in a visual metaphor of squirting.

"Good," she said. "Do that, but even *more*."

I flopped my arms to my sides and laughed uncomfortably. I fixed my hair. I'm still cool, I reminded myself. This was her idea, not mine.

"All right, let's try something else. Tell me, what would an erection say, if it could talk?"

"I don't know . . . this is hard," I said, smirking.

"Close your eyes and forget everything you are," she said. "Your name is not Micah, you are not a human being. You are an erection. What words come into your head?"

I did as she said, closed my eyes. A five-foot-eleven erection, I thought to myself, imagining a layer of thick, pink skin wrapped around my body like a sleeping bag, a giant bulging head.

"This is gross."

"It might help if you stood up straight," she suggested. "As straight as you possibly can."

I shook off the vision, pulled back my shoulders, gritted my teeth, and stiffened all the muscles in my body.

"You do not have a penis," my mother said—to my sudden alarm—"but you *are* the penis. Let its essence fill you."

I sucked in air, pulled my chin up high, and began to see moving red shapes, like blood cells rushing around inside my eyes. It was probably just the sun dappling through the branches, but I was willing to go with it. I imagined them filling me up from head to toe, transforming me into a giant hard-on.

"Yes!" my mother cheered, sensing it was starting to work.

"Um . . . move out of my way," I said, "I'm coming through."

"That's *good*," she encouraged. "Here, I'll be the obstacle. Try to get through me."

She squared her feet against the ground, braced her hands against my shoulders. I opened my eyes and leaned into her, gently at first, but she was seriously resisting, so I pushed harder until we were butting up against each other like two linebackers. "You're not going anywhere!" she shouted.

I launched forward, throwing my shoulder into her chest, but she held me at bay. My face grew crimson, veins popping out from my neck.

"What do you say?!" she shouted. I recognized what I was supposed to do next; it'd been drilled into me since I was a kid. I even knew the psychological term for it: *amplify*.

"I go for what I want at all costs," I answered, my voice rising. "I have just *one* need, and my whole purpose is to fulfill it." As my strength grew, her hold faltered.

"You will not distract me!" I shoved my mother onto the grass, sprinting into the park, arms in the air. I was the victorious penis!

What I'd won, I wasn't sure.

I shuffled back over to where she stood brushing grass off her shirt. "How is this going to make any difference?" I asked and looked between my legs, imagining my guy down there, hiding away.

"Try not to focus on that," she said, glancing vaguely toward my pants, "and just *be* it." She stood up straight like a soldier and furrowed her brow, mimicking my imitation of an erection. "Out of my way! I know what I want," she said, leaning in to check me with her shoulder.

———

My chance to "be" an erection came sooner than I thought, but not exactly in the way I was expecting. It started with the old green manual typewriter that my father bought for me from a yard sale and on which I wrote my first memoirs about getting hit by a car when I was eight years old. The typewriter smelled sharply of ink and the letter *j* didn't work, so I had to write each one in with a pencil. I stopped using it when my parents bought our first computer, but I kept it under my bed.

One night, drinking fuzzy navels with my best friend Jacob, I dragged out the typewriter.

"I used to write on this when I was little," I said, and hit a few random letters. I rolled a piece of paper into it and wrote: "Jacob, I am fucking drunk." Oddly, the *j* was working again in Jacob's presence.

I turned the typewriter toward him. Jacob returned the sentiment but with more emphasis (he's always been a bit of a drama queen): "I AM FUCKING DRUNK AS SHIT."

The truth was we weren't *that* drunk. But drunk enough, apparently, for me to write: "I want to fuck."

Jacob took his turn: "Fucking is good." (*He* knew this from personal experience, whereas I could still only imagine.)

Back to me: "If you were a girl, I would fuck you."

Jacob wrote: "Me too."

And that was that. We were not girls, after all, neither one of us. We finished our fuzzy navels, got stoned, didn't really know what we were going to do that night. We'd abandoned many of our other friends over the previous months to spend more and more time alone together.

We decided before making any decisions we needed to get more drunk. I went under the sink where my father kept his alcohol, pulled out a giant plastic bottle of whiskey, opened it, and passed it to Jacob. He took a long swig, coughed, and then passed it back. We kept going that way, neither one of us wanting to call it quits until at some point we were both lying down on the

kitchen floor, the bottle idle between us. After several minutes—
or half an hour—of that, I started climbing the cabinet below the
sink like it was one of the Rocky Mountains.

"The counter . . . is so far away," I said, stretching my arm and
finally grasping it, evolving myself back into a modern humanoid.
I gave Jacob my hand, and, only partially dislocating his shoulder, got him back on his feet as well. A minute of recovering our
balance later, we felt much better. I headed to the stereo and
put on my father's five-disc changer. We rocked out to George
Michael's "Faith." And wouldn't you know it, suddenly we were
great dancers!

"Tonight," one of us proclaimed, "we should just do whatever
we want."

"Whatever we want!" the other called out.

"No matter what it is, we should do it."

"Just do it!"

Suddenly, the evening and our entire lives seemed to lie ahead
of us and it was going to be a great life. It was going to be awesome. I thought about how much I loved Jacob, something I'd
even told him several times over the last months. He'd said that
he loved me too. Although his dark hair, brown eyes, and soft
oval face made us obviously not kin, we called each other *soul
brothers*.

Then we made eye contact and it was mutually known. Blood
rushed to my face and adrenaline surged through me. I remembered what my mother had said in the park only a couple weeks
before: You have to *be* the erection in your life.

That night, everything worked, but I hadn't even tried to make
it work—it just did all by itself.

Jung was not overly concerned with homosexuality, by which I mean he never took it on as a topic directly. When he did write about it, it was usually secondary subject matter coincidentally brought up in a paper on something else. One Jungian analyst, Robert Hopcke, wrote a book called *Jung, Jungians & Homosexuality,* in which he goes through Jung's references to homosexuality one by one, basically illustrating that Jung's views were somewhat varied over the span of his career. But one thing Jung kept coming back to was the insistence that it was a son's overattachment to his mother after adolescence—not sexual, mind you, but emotional—that ultimately caused him to be homosexual and not develop into a "normal" man. (I could find no Jungian references, incidentally, about the homosexual-inducing influence of a teenage boy's mother telling him to become an erection.)

Jacob is the only guy I ever had a sexual relationship with (it lasted almost two years), but after reading Jung's point of view, my first love does appear to be a textbook example of how mother-son closeness leads to homosexuality. That's an analysis I would accept more readily, however, if Jung hadn't also at times viewed being gay as a kind of mental disorder.

While writing about the interpretation of dreams, Jung described one of his clients, a man in his early twenties. He says the man possessed "a touch of girlishness in his looks and manner of expression." Further, he observed that the young man had "pronounced intellectual and aesthetic interests" and a "fine appreciation of art in all forms." Jung doesn't mince words in his diagnosis: "Undoubtedly he is too young for his age, a clear case of retarded development. It is quite in keeping with this that he should have come to me on account of his homosexuality."

To be fair, the young man in question came to Jung explicitly asking him to "cure" him of his homosexuality. In one of the client's dreams, he is in a cathedral and is about to be ceremoniously lowered down into a dark well. "As in nearly all cases of this kind, he had a particularly close tie with his mother," Jung observes, interpreting the presence of the church in the dream as a substitution for the mother.

In a follow-up dream, the client again is in a cathedral, this time with his real-life gay lover. A priest is with them and is going to baptize a small ivory figure that the dreamer is holding, which the client tells Jung is a stand-in for his own penis. Then, an elderly woman who reminds the client of his mother enters and takes a fraternity ring off the lover's finger and places it on her own. After explaining that the presence of the male priest represents the client's unconscious wish to be inducted into the "world of adult men"—which he is currently refusing by being homosexual— Jung commends the client's unconscious for moving the ring over to a woman's hand. Jung says that even though the woman reminds the client of his mother, she "is not his mother any longer, so the relationship with her signifies a step beyond the mother towards masculinity, and hence a partial conquest of his adolescent homosexuality."

In our current time, in which homosexuality is more accepted and increasingly is being integrated into the mainstream, the problem with this generalization is that, if you ask around, not all gay men are that attached to their mothers. Some are markedly *detached* from them, just as I suppose straight guys are supposed to be, though obviously not all of them are. Jung was aware of the fact that a neurosis could be created in part by the negative judgments of the supposed scientific authority and culture of the time, but his analysis makes it apparent that even he couldn't escape falling into the negative judgment of the time in which he lived.

Jung also once spoke of homosexuality in the context of Nazi Germany. He was asked during an interview shortly before Germany's unconditional surrender in 1945 what the consequences would be to the German psyche when the war ended, and he began by explaining the reasons Germany got into the mess in the first place. "Of all the Western peoples, they were the ones who, at the general exodus from the Eastern womb of the nations, remained too long with their mother. Finally they did get out, but arrived too late. . . . Hence the Germans are profoundly troubled with a national inferiority complex, which they try to compensate by megalomania. . . . It is a typical adolescent psychology, apparent . . . in the extraordinary prevalence of homosexuality."

Later, for good measure, Jung added that "Ten per cent of the German population today are hopeless psychopaths."

According to both Freud and Jung, the consequence of not detaching from one's parents was not just the "disorder" of homosexuality, but a generalized dysfunction, which they called neurosis. As much as I searched through their writings for a clear definition of the term, it seems to be something of a catch-all, including persistent anxiety and phobias; inability to make decisions for oneself and form adult romantic relationships; and so on. The neurotic avoids growing up and making the difficult adult decisions we have to make on a daily basis by clinging instead to the memory of the ease of early life when one's parents helped fulfill one's needs. So instead of realizing he is a capable and strong adult, the neurotic suffering from an Oedipal attachment thinks he's weak. Then, it becomes something of a self-fulfilling prophecy.

Jung's cautionary advice was this: "[T]he child has become closely attached to the family by his whole previous history, and especially to the parents, so that it is often only with the greatest difficulty that the growing individual can free himself inwardly from his infantile milieu. If he does not succeed in this, the Oedipus (or Electra) complex will precipitate a conflict, and then there is the possibility of neurotic disturbances."

My own efforts to free myself from the "infantile milieu" had the additional burden of my mother being a psychologist, a complication Jung might not have imagined in the early days of therapy, when women were usually the patients and not the doctors.

During my last year of university, I invited my girlfriend Beth to come home with me for Christmas. Because we'd only been together then for a few months, I thought she would decline. When she promptly purchased an airline ticket, I started to get nervous, though I couldn't say exactly why at first.

Beth flew in a couple days after I did, so when I picked her up at the airport, I'd already acclimatized to being back home. I often found when I went home the first couple years after heading off to university, I quickly felt like a child again. Sometimes, as my mother would make me breakfast or my father would drive me around doing errands, I'd think about my independent life back at university and have a hard time believing that it really existed. Did I really make decisions on a daily basis about my life, function on my own, and carry on adult relationships? Waking up in my parents' houses and being fed breakfast by them, it was hard to remember how I was managing all that.

I think this is why, when I first saw Beth coming off the plane, she was almost unrecognizable to me. All of the parts of her face which I had come to know as Beth were present—her smiling green eyes, the smooth roundness of her pale skin, her punkish bleached-blonde hair—but were seemingly all in a different order and in different places. I was somewhat relieved when she told me she was experiencing the same thing and later we joked about our "cubist reunion."

In Montreal, at university, our relationship made sense. At home, it did not. Our relationship hadn't changed, but just the rules of the environment. My mother and I were used to sitting around for hours at a time talking about the finer points of our psyches, something Beth and I didn't do. We did talk about things, but together, we were less interested in *what was happening* inside of us, and instead would go out into the world to see what was happening out there.

One afternoon during Beth's visit, after we'd spent the whole morning inside talking with my mother in the kitchen, Beth suddenly jumped up and rushed to the living room window.

"It's snowing!" she cried out joyfully.

I got up slowly and dragged myself to her side. *Oh, here she goes getting all excited about something superficial.* (This was me thinking, but it was the me sunk back into the maternal nest.)

"Yes, you're right," I said. "It is."

"Let's go out there! Let's walk in the snow!"

I said sure, found my coat, and slowly laced up my boots while Beth waited by the door.

"Mom," I called out toward the kitchen, where she was still seated.

"Yes?"

"We're going out for a walk. We'll be back in a little while."

"Okay."

Beth pulled open the door and jumped out into the fresh snow.

"It's amazing," she said when we'd gotten out to the sidewalk. "We are the first people to walk on this snow. No one else has touched it. It's completely ours."

"All ours," I mumbled. It was snow that had just fallen. I didn't see what was so amazing about that.

Beth started running around, kicking the snow, putting handfuls of it in her mouth.

I dragged my boots in the street to spell a word.

"Fuck!" Beth yelled when she saw it. That was the word I had spelled. She grabbed my hand and tried to get me to run with her. I played along, but lagged behind.

She stopped and looked me in the eye. "What's wrong?" she asked.

"Nothing's wrong."

Beth turned her head to the sky. "It's so beautiful," she said. "Look up."

I looked up. Snow fell on my face like cold darts. I turned to her. "It's just . . . I worry that you and my family don't get along."

"We're getting along, aren't we?"

"I guess." I thought for a moment. "Maybe it's something I need to talk to my mom about."

"We can talk about it," she said.

"I know, but it might be better just to talk about it with her when we get back. We can all talk about it."

"Okay," Beth agreed and went running off to make more tracks.

When we got back, Beth and I and my mother found a quiet place to sit, in the room with the piano which also served as my mother's home office. We all sat on pillows on the ground.

"So what's happening?" my mother asked.

"I'll start," I said. "Being home is making me worry that Beth and I are not the right people for each other. And I'm also worried that you don't like her." That first bit would have been the first time Beth had heard about my doubts and hearing it that way, in front of my mother, I can imagine now was probably not so awesome for her. Luckily, my mother quickly distracted us with a positive exclamation.

"But I do like Beth!" she said. She then turned to Beth—who was remaining remarkably well-composed—and asked her how she was feeling. Beth told my mother how much she loved me and that she hoped my family would like her. Her honesty was endearing. I moved over to her and we put our arms around each other.

"That's a good sign that you guys are moving closer together," my mother said. "It's very cute." Then she dropped the Oedipal bomb. "You know," she said, looking at me, "I have realized over the last few days that I'm a little sad that I'm no longer the primary person in your life."

I was used to frankness from my mother, but this admission silenced me. It felt like my mother had lifted a veil that was not supposed to be lifted. I too felt this loss, but I would never have spoken of it.

"But," she continued, "I know that this is the right thing to happen."

"That's very brave of you to admit," Beth said.

I was relieved that Beth didn't freak out, and the rest of the trip went a lot better. I once again recognized Beth and the reasons I liked her, which were different from the reasons I liked my mother.

———

Recently, as I was reading Jung's memoir, I was intrigued to learn about one of his clients whom he thought suffered from an unhealthy Oedipal attachment to his mother. The man came to Jung because he had a serious drinking problem. "His mother was the owner of a large company, and the unusually talented son occupied a leading post in the firm," Jung writes, explaining that he "remained chained to his mother, who had installed him in the business." The drinking, Jung concluded, was a self-medication to numb him from his fate of surviving permanently under his mother's thumb. "A part of him did not really want to leave the comfortably warm nest, and against his own instincts he was allowing himself to be seduced by wealth and comfort," he wrote.

The case Jung presented reminded me of something that happened when I was fourteen. I had written a short story for school about a boy who, while his parents are away one day, runs into the woods behind his house and gets lost. The boy has many adventures, becomes injured, loses his trail of flour in the rain, but eventually finds his way home by a river. Looking back now, the story reads like my very own archetypal allegory of a boy becoming a man, becoming independent and self-sufficient from his parents, taking his life into his own hands. I wrote this masterpiece in a flurry over a weekend and I was quite proud of it. I showed it to my mother when I was done and after lavishing some praise on the story she informed me that it contained some grammatical errors that she could fix if I wanted. I said sure.

When she was done, I sat back down at the computer and read my story. But it wasn't my story anymore. The plot was the same, but the rhythm had changed, words were different. My voice was broken. Maybe I was a budding precious writer, but my mother had left no marks of the corrections, so essentially she had overwritten my story. Since my mother is not a monster, however, when I burst into tears, she was sent into a panic and restored the story as best she could, grammatical mistakes included.

In the case of Jung's client, the situation was resolved when Jung took a drastic and, by his own admission, somewhat unethical action. Jung had the mother come in to see him. "She was an intelligent woman, but was a real 'power devil,'" Jung says. "I saw what the son had to contend with, and realized that he did not have the strength to resist. Physically, too, he was rather delicate and no match for his mother."

Jung's scam was to present the mother with a "medical certificate to the effect that her son's alcoholism rendered him incapable of fulfilling the requirements of his job." So essentially, Jung used his authority to advise the mother to fire her son, which she did. Jung's client was angry with him, but not too long afterward, was cured. "His wife was grateful to me," says Jung, "for her husband had not only overcome his alcoholism, but had also struck out on his own individual path with the greatest success."

Interestingly, despite all of Freud and Jung's concerns with parent-child attachments, both fathers of psychology fell victim to tricky Electra complexes—as the father-daughter bond was called—in their own lives.

Freud held so tightly to his youngest daughter Anna—whom he continued calling his "little one" into adulthood—that she never married. Although he continually expressed concern about her single status, he also did things to prevent her from forming intimate connections with men, such as the time when he warned his protege Ernest Jones to not touch her because she was not ready for a relationship. This happened when she was nineteen. Meanwhile, Jung's daughter Marianne, who did end up having a family of her own, clung to Jung at his deathbed. According to Deirdre Bair's biography, Marianne wouldn't permit a professional nurse to take care of him and insisted on doing it herself. "Her children thought the bond between the dying father and the desperately ill daughter was eerie, and that the willpower of each held the other to life as if by a tenuous thread," writes Bair. Finally, Jung's health became bad enough that Marianne succumbed and hired a nurse. Marianne still stayed by his side, however, and only reluctantly left when she had a doctor's appointment she absolutely had to go to. "When the beloved went away," Marianne's son Rudolf told Bair, "then he could die." And he did.

A couple years after her first visit to Colorado, Beth visited again. In the middle of the trip, we went with my mother and Peter to a coffeehouse and about ten minutes after sitting down, we somehow got on the topic of incest. What, doesn't it always come up?

"When girls are sexually abused by their fathers, they get depressed and are usually sexually messed up," my mother said during the discussion. "But when boys are sexually abused by their mothers, they become psychotic."

I noticed after she said this that Beth was starting to look uncomfortable. Maybe any conversation about incest with people you'd only met once before would be odd, but I knew another reason Beth was upset: I had told her during our courtship about the unfortunate vision I'd had when I was fifteen. I thought back then it made for entertaining conversation, but it also opened up an Oedipal Pandora's box. I wasn't exactly a mama's boy anymore, but I was still very close to my mother, something that could make Beth feel insecure.

I tried to think of a conversational tangent away from incest as quickly as possible. But where exactly can you go from that? I couldn't think fast enough.

"I kind of feel like taking a walk," Beth interrupted. "But you guys stay, I'm just going to go for a walk."

Freud can really make one paranoid. He and Jung worried so much about the neuroses caused by the relationship to the mother that they almost appear, well, neurotic about it. Certainly, a son needs to go off into the world and meet another woman to mate with, but does that necessarily mean he must think of this new woman as a substitute for his mother?

Jung did eventually change his tune somewhat. After he split with Freud, he maintained that what his mentor had discovered about the Oedipal onset of neurosis was not incorrect, but that it was simply just one piece of the puzzle. The draw of the mother and the toppling of the father was one storyline among hundreds, thousands. Then Jung was off down the road toward bringing more spiritual matters into psychology, something Freud's sexual theory disallowed and a path which Jung seemed to feel compelled to defend to the end of his life.

"Above all, Freud's attitude toward the spirit seemed to me highly questionable," Jung wrote in his memoir. "Wherever, in a person or in a work of art, an expression of spirituality (in the intellectual, not the supernatural sense) came to light, he suspected it, and insinuated that it was repressed sexuality. Anything that could not be directly interpreted as sexuality he referred to as 'psychosexuality.' I protested that this hypothesis, carried to its logical conclusion, would lead to an annihilating judgment upon culture. Culture would then appear as a mere farce, the morbid consequence of repressed sexuality. 'Yes,' he assented, 'so it is, and that is just the curse of fate against which we are powerless to contend.'"

A few years ago, in Montreal on vacation, I came across a book called *Oedipus Variations,* which includes an essay by James Hillman, a prominent Jungian.

"Freud emphasizes parricide, both in regard to the Oedipal urge and to the primal horde, where sons kill the father," Hillman writes. "He says less about infanticide, about fathers killing sons. This desire in the father to kill the child we ignore to our peril, especially since psychoanalysis descends from fathers."

Yeah, what about that? Freud spilled so much ink discussing the pathology of a murderous son, but what about the fact that in the beginning of the story, Oedipus's father sent said son off to be killed once he heard the prophecy that Oedipus was going to kill him when he grew up? This dubious action was what began the whole tragedy to begin with.

Hillman's argument is that Freud and Jung's overlooking of this aspect of the myth—which he attributes to the fact that they were the "fathers" of psychoanalysis—leads them to act like Oedipus's father in the way they propagate their ideas. He suggests that Freud and Jung focused too much attention on the Oedipus myth when considering family dynamics and "murdered" the possibility for a next generation of ideas to be born. Freud was intolerant of Jung's later, more metaphysical ideas and once Jung broke free from Freud, he tended to treat his followers with the same narrow-minded obstinance he had been subjected to by Freud. Hillman wonders what psychoanalysis would have looked like if its foundation had been more open to other angles and not solely tied into just one myth: "Would we imagine therapy differently— say, as a work in love with the mythologem of Eros and Psyche paramount; or as a work in generativity and marriage with the myths of Zeus and Hera and their struggles and their progeny; or as a work in imaginative flying and crafting with Icarus and Daedalus; or of Ares and the world of combat, anger, and destruction; or as a world of mimesis where art becomes life through desire with Pygmalion; or a work in which Hermes and Aphrodite or Persephone or Dionysos play the principal—therapy's method would display an altogether different nature."

If Hillman is right, it is the very fact that we focus on the Oedipus-based fear that there is something wrong with mother-son closeness that causes the closeness to become problematic. Instead, it could be healthier for one to consider other mythological models, where such a relationship doesn't lead to tragedy.

I remember the first time I became aware of the form of attraction now commonly and tenderly referred to as "Moms I'd Like to Fuck." My friend Randy and I were sixteen, throwing a football in the road in front of his house. He lived in an upper-class neighborhood populated by lawyers, doctors, and many women who had the luxury of staying home with their babies and keeping fit in their spare time. One such woman—early thirties, blonde, possessing a well-shaped bottom pleasingly displayed in tight sweatpants—wheeled her stroller by our game of catch. Randy turned around to gawk at her.

"There's nothing more attractive than a hot mom," he said once she was out of hearing range. "She gave birth. She had a baby, and she's *still* hot," he said, shaking his head.

This woman was certainly not the hottest female to cross our path that day, but for Randy, the hotness that she did possess was heightened by the sheer sweat and pain that she had gone through to propagate life and then the seemingly superhuman commitment it would take to become once again so hot in such a short period of time. This idea of a woman going through such an ordeal and the strength that she must have had to do it turned Randy on.

"She doesn't look like she's had a baby at all," he said.

And yet the evidence was there, irrefutable, dripping saliva on its chin.

"That baby has a hot mom," he stated finally, then passed the ball to me.

I had to agree.

I like to think of the MILF phenomenon not just as a perverted niche objectification of women—though it is that—but also as one of the signs that, after half a century of viewing mothers and motherhood not so highly, we might be starting to see them with more respect. Part of what makes the MILF attractive is that she is a *mother*. Not only is she hot, and you'd like to have sex with her, but she's also a caretaker, a symbol of fertility. Wanting to have sex with the idea of the mother might sound like a Freudian-style regression, but it could also be that we're simply changing the focus of our feelings for mothers away from fear and are therefore less at risk of actually regressing.

My mother once told me that when people we know appear in our dreams, it can mean two different things. Sometimes, she said, the dream is literally about that person in the dream. The dreamer may be seeing some essential truth about that person or playing out some dynamic of the real-world relationship with the dream object. More commonly, however, she says the person in the dream represents an aspect of the dreamer's own psyche. So if I have a dream about one of my close friends, my mother would ask me to describe that person. Adventurous, I might say. That friend goes into situations without fear. She'd say then that the figure in the dream represents the part of me that is adventurous and is urging me to take more risks.

So let's lay me down on the couch and look at my unfortunate vision—which is close enough to a dream as far as analysis is concerned. Freud would say that this should be looked at as a literal wish fulfillment. My mother popped into my head because I wanted to consummate my desire for her in a fantasy since, in the real world, the taboo and societal pressures stopped me from getting it on with her.

But what about the other option, the symbolic one? To get at that, I would just need to come up with an adjective or two to describe my mother to figure out what part of my own psyche I need to metaphorically make love to.

That shouldn't be too hard.

4

Anima

(Getting Laid the Jungian Way)

I was sitting with my friend William on his porch, sharing a cigarette after a night hanging out with friends during my first summer home from university.

"Well, did you at least come on her?" he asked.

I tried to picture it, doing that to Sarah, high atop the pedestal on which she was placed, her long blonde hair falling around her pale cheeks and pouting lips as she gazed down at me with her blue eyes framed with charcoal.

"No," I said. "I didn't do that." At the time, the suggestion seemed crude. One did not do such things to Sarah.

I had just told William that, although I had been dating Sarah for the last five months and had ended up spending the night at her place a few times, we had not had sex. Thus, going on twenty, I was still, as far as women are concerned, a virgin.

When I met Sarah, Jacob and I were still together. After carrying on our relationship covertly at the end of high school, we had gone to the same university. Although we agreed that we would make an effort to go our separate ways, after a couple days we were hanging out as much as usual and, once again, carrying on in secret.

The first time I saw Sarah she was sitting on the floor in the library, her knees pulled up to her chest, reading Simone de Beauvoir. Wearing jeans and resting on the drab gray carpet of the soulless building, she seemed normal enough, just another freshman pursuing an arts degree. The first time she invited me into her room, though, I realized she was unique. On my dorm room wall, a poster of Einstein declared "Imagination is more important than knowledge," which, since it was the same poster hanging in one out of every three dorm rooms, was the most unimaginative wall decoration possible. Sarah's room, on the other hand, was covered with fierce sketches of half-dressed women that she had drawn herself with burnt orange charcoals. Egon Schiele's mottled prostitute adorned a post-card above her bed.

I began spending as much time in that room as I could, visits during which she often spoke in cryptic phrases that I could not decipher. Sometimes, she would read me poetry and laugh during parts that weren't funny. She responded to simple questions with long stories that didn't end up answering the question at all. The more I got to know Sarah, the more I realized she was a little, well, crazy. Eccentric, at least. And so, no doubt rebelling against having grown up in a family where mental orderliness and honest communication were of the utmost importance, I promptly fell in love with her.

According to Jung, after a man comes through the Oedipus complex (mostly) unscathed, he has another obstacle to face and that is the *anima*. Jung thought all men had an inner woman, a container for his feminine qualities and the home of something he called "feelings." In his conscious life, a man is busy doing things, making decisions, being logical, but inside of him his anima is experiencing emotions. Freud had a similar theory but explained the phenomenon in evolutionary terms: we were all hermaphrodites way, way back, he pointed out, and thus retained traces of the other sex. Jung's take is more philosophical, akin to the Taoist concept of yin and yang. Everything in the universe is a union of opposites, he thought, even individuals.

I'd once told my mother about a dream I had where I was running arm in arm with a girl my age through the streets of some unknown city. Being with this girl made me feel alive and in the dream I was in love with her.

"Why can't I just meet this girl in real life?" I asked my mother.

"Because she's not real," she said. "She's your anima. She's part of you—your feeling side."

According to Jung, the anima not only pervades a man's literal dreams, but also his fantasies, the ones that just naturally fill his head during boring moments at boardroom meetings or while roaming aisles at the supermarket. "She is not an invention of the conscious," he wrote, "but a spontaneous product of the unconscious."

Jung eventually decided women have a similar thing going on, which he called the *animus*—the man inside a woman. A woman, he thought, was preoccupied mostly with feelings and relationships in her conscious life, so her animus was an action-oriented figure—one who can get things done and is forceful about opinions.

To complicate matters, Jung also decided that a man's inner woman had an inner man and a woman's inner man an inner woman. This could make men become aggressively emotional or women irrationally stubborn. "Men can argue in a very womanish way, too, when they are anima-possessed and have thus been transformed into the animus of their own anima," he explained. "With them the question becomes one of personal vanity and touchiness (as if they were females); with women it is a question of *power*, whether of truth or justice or some other 'ism'—for the dressmaker and the hairdresser have already taken care of their vanity."

Now, although a man's inner woman is inside him, she often appears outside him when he projects her onto women he meets. When this happens, he's not actually seeing the person in front of him, but a fantasy.

"There are certain types of women who seem to be made by nature to attract anima projections; indeed one could almost speak of a definite 'anima type,'" wrote Jung. "The so-called 'sphinx-like' character is an indispensable part of their equipment, also an equivocalness, an intriguing elusiveness—not an indefinite blur that offers nothing, but an indefiniteness that seems full of promises, like the speaking silence of a Mona Lisa. A woman of this kind is both old and young, mother and daughter, of more than doubtful chastity, childlike, and yet endowed with a naïve cunning that is extremely disarming to men."

A hundred years before Sarah was even born, he had my delusional fantasy of her nailed.

———————

I was lying on my bed, attempting to sketch yet another portrait of Sarah's face with my amateur artistic skills, when the phone rang.

"Hello, Honey." It was her. She hadn't called in a week, during which I had left her three unanswered voice messages, as well as one with her roommate who informed me that, yes, she had received *all* the previous ones.

"Where are you?" I asked, breathless. She told me she was at a café about a fifteen-minute walk away.

"If you can make it here in ten minutes, I'll still be here," she said and hung up. I threw on my black turtleneck and fixed my hair. Should I wear the cape, I wondered? Yes! I buttoned on the cape I'd picked up at a secondhand shop the week before. It was a nurse's cape but since nurses didn't wear capes anymore, I had decided that nobody would recognize it as such and instead it would serve as a close enough imitation of what Lord Byron would have worn in Britain at the turn of the nineteenth century and would thus transform me into an appropriate image of Sarah's lover.

I bolted from my room and sprinted across the grounds to make it to the café before she vanished.

When I arrived, Sarah had finished her drink and just as I was sitting down she stood up.

"I need a cucumber," she told me.

"Right," I said, following her out. She put her arm through mine as we walked.

"I'm going to make you dinner," she said. "And then maybe you can spend the night."'

I was thrilled.

We made conversation and I tried to talk about things worthy of her: art, poetry, philosophy. I avoided talking about anything as silly as school or the relatively conventional people who lived in my dorm—the things that predominantly made up my life. No reference was made to the fact that I was wearing a nurse's cape.

At the first greengrocer we visited, Sarah picked up a cucumber and called across the store to the man at the counter: "From where does this cucumber come?"

The man shrugged.

"Well you should find out!" she shouted angrily, then broke into giggles. She put the cucumber back down and as we passed the man to leave she leaned over and kissed him on the cheek. "I love you," she said.

"Where oh where am I going to find the right cucumber to fill me up?" she called out into the street, giggling again.

"So what are you going to make for dinner?" I asked. She stopped suddenly in her tracks.

"Look," she said, "I have to go now. It was lovely to see you."

We had spent about twenty minutes together.

"But, aren't I coming over?"

"I don't think so, Sweetie." She waved her arm for a taxi. One pulled over. "I have to go," she said. Then she kissed me on the cheek, jumped in the back seat and was gone.

My time with Sarah was a blur of similarly strange errands and more unanswered phone calls, relieved in brief moments where we would actually sit down together and converse or drink wine before making out on her futon. As a friend kindly put it to me after I recounted such events: "That girl has you whipped."

She was an artist. I forgave her.

Several women in Jung's life likely influenced his conception of the anima. He said in some recorded but unpublished conversations that the anima was directly influenced by a woman named Maria Moltzer, whom he met when she was an assistant at the Zurich mental hospital where he worked at the beginning of his career. "She was intense, intellectual, and driven, and Jung was so physically attracted to her that he called her the first inspiration for his formulation of the anima, the inner female configuration within the male," writes his biographer Deirdre Bair.

Over the years, however, others have suggested there was another model for the anima and that is a woman named Sabina Spielrein. Like Moltzer, Jung met Spielrein at the hospital, only she wasn't an assistant but his patient. Jung met the twenty-year-old when she was brought to the Burghölzli with an acute neurosis stemming from being spanked by her father, an experience that, according to Jung, brought her pleasure.

As Jung worked with Spielrein, he quickly found himself attracted to her. She was dark, mysterious, intellectual—the very opposite of his wife, Emma, who was sturdy and practical, eminently sane. When Jung realized that he was not able to control his feelings for Spielrein, he broke off his doctor-patient relationship with her and transitioned to a friendship that carried on for a few years, during which time they may or may not have had an affair. No one has been able to prove it is true, but Spielrein herself started going around Zurich claiming she was Jung's lover.

Jung and Freud wrote a series of letters back and forth during this time. Jung claimed that, from the beginning, Spielrein was "systematically planning my seduction." According to Jung, he didn't succumb to these advances but because she was able to open up a deep mysterious longing in him, he broke off their friendship just as earlier he had ended their therapeutic relationship. Shortly after that, a rumor was spread around Zurich that Jung was planning to divorce his wife. Jung jumped to the conclusion that it was Spielrein who had spread the gossip. "Now she is seeking revenge," Jung wrote to Freud. In a response, Freud marveled at the seductive power of the female: "The way these women manage to charm us with every conceivable psychic perfection until they have attained their purpose is one of nature's greatest spectacles."

Years later, when Jung wrote in his memoir about the first time his anima spoke to him and described it as the voice of "a talented psychopath who had a strong transference to me," he likely meant Spielrein. At the time he heard the voice he was working on some creative writing and this voice told him that it was "art." For a moment, he felt proud of himself for this inner woman's appraisal of his work, but then immediately started to question her motivations. Now she was saying he was an artist, Jung thought, but since the voice came from the irrational emotion-based part inside him, she could easily later call him a fool for thinking it was art and could damage his ego. "Thus the insinuations of the anima, the mouthpiece of the unconscious, can utterly destroy a man," he concluded.

─────────────

It should have been clear to me that there was something not quite sane about my obsession with Sarah when I found myself comparing her to a black widow spider. During a summer night back home from university and away from Sarah, my friends and I were hanging out and had spontaneously invented a drinking game. We had a deck of cards with drawings of animals on each. As we went around, each person would pull two cards randomly from the deck and then say which animal they'd rather have sex with. After someone was forced to choose between a parrot and a blue whale, we realized this was ridiculous, so we changed the game so that you had to choose between two human beings who possessed the traits of the animals shown. (As if this was somehow less ridiculous!) Drinking was part of it, I don't remember how, but we must have been drunk to have made it up in the first place. After a player had made his or her decision, other players were allowed to debate the choice.

It came to my turn. I flipped two cards: a dog and a black widow spider. I knew right away which one I wanted to have sex with.

"Spider," I said.

Jacob spat out his beer. "What!? Why would you pick a spider over a dog?"

"Spiders are kind of sexy," I insisted. "Dogs are all slobbery."

"A black widow kills its mate!" he shouted as if I'd personally offended him.

"Well, danger can be kind of hot," I shot back.

Our other friends were silent and utterly confused.

"Dogs are loyal and fun loving," Jacob returned. "You can't be serious that you'd rather be with someone who, after you have sex with them, is going to *kill* you."

"It's just a metaphor!"

"Yes, it is a metaphor, Micah. And when presented with a choice of metaphors, you choose the one that is cold, evil, and will poison you over one who is loyal and cute."

"I'm staying with the spider."

"That's retarded." Jacob had had enough of the conversation, put down his drink and took off. I just shrugged to the rest of my friends and we kept on drinking, though we abandoned the soured game.

William sat with me outside after everyone else had left.

"You know, I have to admit," he said, "dogs *are* cute and really lovable."

"I know," I said.

"So have you had sex with Sarah yet, or what?"

That's when I admitted that I had not and that, no, I had not
even come on her.

That summer, I often fantasized about Sarah. I'd close my eyes
and imagine her walking toward me in a long black dress. We'd
of course be standing at the edge of a cliff above the ocean, the
wind violently threatening to knock us over. (What's a fantasy
without a little dramatic embellishment?) As she came closer to
me, I'd reach out toward her, my cape streaming behind me, but
before I could touch her, she would dissolve into a black mist or
fly apart into a swarm of insects. I'd open my eyes and curse my
uncooperative unconscious.

———————————

The thing about the anima is that she is not and cannot be a
real person, but only a form, a container, an empty Jell-O mold.
"Every man carries within him the eternal image of woman,"
wrote Jung, "not the image of this or that particular woman, but
a definitive feminine image. This image is fundamentally unconscious, an hereditary factor of primordial origin engraved in the
living organic system of the man, an imprint or 'archetype' of all
the ancestral experiences of the female, a deposit, as it were, of
all the impressions ever made by woman." So according to Jung,
when a man gazes at a woman strutting down the street, he's

not just looking at that one woman, he's looking at thousands of women, the whole goddamn history of them.

Now, go up to that woman and start talking to her and the fantasy is destroyed because, as it turns out, a woman is a real person with individual characteristics and motivations.

Interestingly, though, Jung did feel that while the anima is a timeless form that is passed on from man to man through generations, early life experiences can deeply impress themselves and give a man's anima at least a degree of uniqueness. In Jung's memoir, he describes his earliest such attraction, which Freud would probably hasten to point out is one of the classic mother substitutes—his maid.

"While my mother was away, our maid, too, looked after me. I still remember her picking me up and laying my head against her shoulder. She had black hair and an olive complexion, and was quite different from my mother. I can see, even now, her hairline, her throat, with its darkly pigmented skin, and her ear. All this seemed to me very strange and yet strangely familiar. It was as though she belonged not to my family but only to me, as though she were connected in some way with other mysterious things I could not understand. This type of girl later became a component of my anima. The feeling of strangeness which she conveyed, and yet of having known her always, was a characteristic of that figure which later came to symbolize for me the whole essence of womanhood."

Jung's account reminds me of my own early memory, a childhood love whom I now refer to as Peanut Butter Girl.

I was four years old, in preschool. During recess, I would watch other kids playing with each other, but for some reason that social interaction didn't interest me. I walked around the playground alone, jumped up and down, ascended and descended the various playground structures.

But one day, I saw a game that did entice me. There was a girl in our class who was sought after by all the boys. She had long blonde hair and rosy cheeks like a fairy tale princess. She was also an extremely fast runner, faster than all the boys. They would chase her around the schoolyard trying to catch her so they could kiss her. I was fast and I loved to run, so I joined the pack. After a little while of sprinting as hard as I could, I found myself in the lead. I was even gaining on her.

When I was within a couple feet, almost in arm's reach, she suddenly stopped and turned around to face me. I leaned in and we kissed on the lips. Even at age 4, I had seen people kiss in a few movies. I thought I knew what it would be like, but I was shocked by the reality. The kiss tasted like peanut butter. I stopped cold, dumbfounded that a princess could taste of something so mundane.

Later, we found each other again inside and we jumped on a giant pillow together. For a day we were like a couple in love. Then, as in all the great tragedies, the two of us were eventually separated by a villain—our teacher—and this time we were not able to find each other again. I remember looking for her, but I was still experiencing the world as a sensory swamp where my memory of faces was short term and only my parents had stable bodies. Even though she was probably sitting nearby, I never found her.

Like Jung's maid, Peanut Butter Girl left a deep impression

on my anima. During lonely times, I've wondered what it would be like to meet her now. (If she's reading this, could she please call me?)

During my summer home from university I was living with my father in Denver, but once again spending many weekends with my mother in Boulder.

"I'm in love," I told my mother during one of our walks. I'd briefly mentioned Sarah over the phone when I was still at school.

"That's good," she said.

"You sound unconvinced."

"Well, you haven't told me much about your relationship with her."

"It's good," I said. "Although . . . we haven't had sex yet." At the time, it seemed like the most pertinent detail.

"Really? Why not?"

"It just never seemed like the right time. And I think she's been hurt by men in the past, so I want to be careful. But I'm worried it will never happen."

"That doesn't sound so good."

"It's fine. I'm just going to be really nice to her and eventually I'm sure it'll work out."

"Hmm, I'm a little concerned, Micah, with the way you're describing her. Does Sarah like men?"

"As a species you mean?"

"Uh huh."

"Well no, not really. She's pretty angry at men. But she's not angry with me."

"You know, if you want to be with a woman, you should first try getting in touch with the woman inside of you." My mother didn't go as far as suggesting that I *be the vagina*, but it seemed like this was the essential message, a sequel to her earlier advice.

"My inner woman?"

"Your anima. Unite with the woman *inside* of you and you will find it easier to be with a woman *outside* of you."

My mother didn't give me any specific instructions on how to achieve the communion with my inner woman, but a couple days later I had a dream while taking a nap in her basement that gave me a clue.

The visuals of the dream were minimal, just a wash of blue and black, but there was a woman's voice—crisp, clear, but also ethereal, like the voice-over of a cheesy fantasy flick from the 1980s: "SHE IS THE TREASURE AND YOU WILL FIND HER IN THE DEEP."

I woke up with that phrase echoing in my ears as if it were being spoken by someone in the room. It was strange to hear a dream voice that loud, saying something nearly cogent. I was startled and disoriented, but stumbled out of my bed to grab a notebook. I had been trained by my parents to capture these fragments, because you never knew when you'd have use for them. Plus, it might just be my inner woman talking, I thought to myself.

"She is the treasure," I wrote in the notebook. "And you will find her in the deep."

I was a Romantic. Literally, I could quote from memory lines from Percy Shelley and William Blake. And did I mention I owned a cape? But even I felt there was something unbearably earnest about what the woman had said to me in my dream. The combination of the word "treasure" as applied to a female, combined with "deep," a word ruined by the hippie generation, was just too much. Was my inner woman really just an untalented poetess?

Later, I would be able to forgive my imagination when reading Jung's explanation of the voices he heard in his head when communicating with his anima. He said she spoke in "high-flown language," and explained that voices from the psyche usually came out in this syrupy form, going on in "the language of high rhetoric, even of bombast. It is a style I find embarrassing; it grates on my nerves, as when someone draws his nails down a plaster wall, or scrapes his knife against a plate. But since I did not know what was going on, I had no choice but to write everything down in the style selected by the unconscious itself."

I too had no choice. It might be my only chance to get laid.

I told my mother about the dream, and she nodded as if it all made sense.

"It's starting to happen," she said.

"It is?"

"Yes."

When I arrived back at school, I was excited to see Sarah again. She was not nearly as excited to see me, a fact that became painfully clear when two weeks passed and she didn't contact me with her new phone number. I had no way to reach her, so I purchased a bicycle and began to roam the area of the city where I might run into her. My roommates must have thought I'd become extremely organized since the previous year, because I went out on an insane number of "errands."

I never found Sarah but she did finally call me. I was on my futon, in a depressive half-nap. When the phone rang I hoped it was her, but was shocked when it actually was. She was at the café down the street from where I lived. She was meeting a friend, but the person wasn't there yet. Did I want to drop by? I changed my shirt, fixed my hair, and headed over.

Seated outside at a table by herself, she was as beautiful as I remembered.

"Hi, Honey," she said, standing up to give me a hug. "Why don't you go get yourself a coffee." I smiled and headed over to the counter, ordering myself a cappuccino. I tried to think of some interesting things to talk about. I didn't have much. I wiped away some sweat from my forehead, breathed deeply, and sat back down.

"Look, I stopped biting my nails," I said. This had been some-thing Sarah complained about before. I held my hand out and she examined.

"That's not good enough," she said. In truth, I had only quit a few days before in order to impress her. "Look, Micah, I have something I need to tell you."

"You do?" It didn't sound promising.

"I'm afraid I'm not looking to have a sexual relationship right now."

I sat silently for a while, mumbled something about the deep-ness of the love I felt for her, but she was unmoved. She brushed some crumbs off the table and said she was sorry. Then the friend showed up and despite the fact I had just had my heart broken for the first time, I pretended nothing had happened.

I spent the next week acting devastated. It's embarrassing to me now to realize how dramatic I was at that age (and still am prob-ably, though I won't know what things to be embarrassed about until ten years from now).

I moped in alleyways. I wrote poetry. One night, I hopped on my bike—the one, I reminded myself with an enormous helping of self-pity, that I had purchased to hunt down Sarah—and ped-aled my way up the mountain in the center of the city. At the top, I let my bike fall to the ground and stood against the railing that overlooks the entire metropolis. I cursed God. Somewhere down there, Sarah walked, ate food, existed.

After some time, when I felt I had mourned my unrequited love for a suitable amount of time, I headed back down. I started thinking about what my mother had said. As much as I didn't want to admit it at the time, I knew all along that Sarah and I weren't going to work. I decided right there and then to see where I could go with this tapping-the-inner-woman deal. Maybe I wasn't embracing my anima enough? Maybe I had to form a sacred union with her first.

"Micah, I keep telling you, you just need to get *laid*." Even though he was still a bit sore about our breakup, Jacob and I were back to being friends.

"I know, but this is how I'm going to do that," I replied.

"What does that even mean—embracing your inner woman? You're making it too complicated. Just find a girl who wants to have sex with you and do it."

"You just don't understand," I told him and ended the conversation.

Jacob was right, of course. If only he had been able to speak the language I was used to hearing, Jungian, he could have put it this way: The reason you never had sex with Sarah was that you never let her just be a real person. She is not some supernaturally sophisticated sphinx, but just another confused eighteen-year-old who knows as little about sex as you do. Unfortunately, her airs of worldliness were met perfectly by your willingness to project them onto her.

That'll be a hundred dollars.

Sarah had once said, "When you look at the moon, think of

me," and I wondered if I would ever be able to wander the streets of the city again when everything, even the moon, would remind me of Sarah.

But as it turns out, I could. After a few weeks of not seeing Sarah at all, I started feeling better. Then, I started to feel even better than better, though I wouldn't be able to say for a while why this was.

On a late fall day, early in the school year, I was walking by a used-book shop near campus and popped in to browse. I already had five books in my arms when I came across *The Goddess Within*. I stopped cold. Yes, I thought, fate has brought me to you. Using you as a guide, I will find my inner woman and have a girlfriend in no time. I took my books to the checkout and headed to meet my friend Heather for coffee.

Like me, Heather had recently been burned by unrequited love, so we'd meet up almost daily to complain and then laugh at ourselves.

When I arrived, she was waiting. She waved and smiled, pushing her unkempt bangs away from her face. I placed my tower of books on the table and started excitedly explaining the reason I bought each one. Heather interrupted me to pull *The Goddess Within* from the bottom of the pile.

"What is this?" she said, turning it over to read the back. "Why did you get this?"

"Oh, that. It's . . . um, part of my quest."

"Your quest?"

"Well, my mom told me that in order to meet the right

woman I had to get in touch with the woman inside myself. So I figured . . ."

She snickered as she flipped through and came to the quiz that tells you which of the goddesses is your personal inner goddess. "Are you going to take this?"

"Yes," I said. "I mean, it won't work if I don't know which goddess I am, right?"

"No, it certainly won't. I'd like to take the quiz when you're done."

I leaned back in my chair. "I buy books when I'm happy," I said.

"You're cute when you're happy."

At home, after my roommates were asleep, I pulled out the goddess book and turned on my bedside lamp. I caught Jung's name on the first page—his ideas were an inspiration for the authors— and I started to read but quickly got restless with all the exposition and went straight to page 324. The quiz. Who doesn't go straight for the quiz?

The goddess quiz asks you to rate eighty-four statements according to how well each one describes you, from "3" for "strongly applies" to "–1" for "not true at all."

First statement: "Since I don't go out a lot, clothes and makeup aren't that important to me." Hmm, I thought, I had put on a bit of eyeliner a couple of times before going out dancing. But I'd done it in a David Bowie way, and I wasn't sure if the authors of The Goddess Within intended that question to be assessing one's inclination to androgynous performance art.

This isn't going to work, I thought, disappointed. But then I looked at the instructions, which I had skipped the first time, and realized the authors had included suggestions for how men should take the quiz. I was supposed to use the same rating system, but instead of applying the statements directly to myself, I was to decide "how much or how little" they "apply to the woman or type of woman" I am most drawn to. Okay, I thought, I can do that. But I was then faced with this conundrum: My ideal woman didn't place very much importance on makeup, but she did like to go out. Why did they have to be connected? Could you not present yourself to the world unless you were covered in foundation and lipstick? Of course, I liked thinking about my ideal woman wearing lipstick and short skirts at home just for me. Was I being possessive in not wanting her to go out like that? I went with a 1.

That was just the beginning. Another one had me stumped: "I mostly loved to play with dolls." Would my ideal woman have liked to play with dolls when she was a girl? My ideal woman would have had more imagination as a girl than to play with Barbies. But then, I did like the idea of having kids someday and maybe playing with dolls was a sign that she would want kids too? I went with a 2.

I bumbled through the rest of the quiz and finally got to the part where you tally up the numbers and find out who your goddess is. Was I going to be Artemis the Huntress? Or would I score Aphrodite, the Golden Goddess of Love, as my inner woman? Not quite. When the final points were calibrated it turned out my inner woman was the most sinister of them all: Persephone, Goddess of the Underworld.

I was psyched about having the wife of Hades as my inner goddess. The book summed her up this way: "The Persephone woman is ruled by the goddess of the underworld; she is mediumistic and is attracted to the spirit world, to the occult, to visionary and mystical experience, and to matters associated with death."

So it was true—my inner woman *was* a flaky poetess!

I skimmed over the chapter more, and it did seem they had me nailed. "We cannot help suspecting that she is more than a little ill at ease with her body and possibly her sexuality," the authors wrote about my inner woman. "In her frailty we sense a yearning for warmth and deep intimacy, though it is often hard to tell whether it is intimacy of the spirit or of the body she really wants." So what were they saying? I didn't really want to get laid? No, I did. But there was that word again—*deep*—haunting me like a curse.

Then the book lost some of its credibility, suggesting that if I experimented with a Ouija board I would realize that I had "all the makings of a medium or a channel."

I closed it and went to sleep. Maybe I'd be able to take advantage of my mediumistic tendencies and at least have an erotic dream.

Heather took the quiz and came out as a Persephone woman as well, but I wasn't sure that she really fit the Goddess of the Underworld bill. She seemed more normal and grounded than that. She made jokes that were actually funny. She laughed. I could imagine her working a day job, something I could never see Sarah doing. Heather drank beer and made lewd comments. She never bolted in the middle of a date. She was a real person and already had a tight relationship with her inner man, which

I suppose made it hard to make any delusional projection of my crazy-girl anima stick.

The funny thing to me now is that, looking back on my childhood, I definitely had not lacked an identification with a feminine side. Having Jungians for parents meant growing up with a certain looseness around gender roles. We're all yin *and* yang, after all.

The bike my parents bought me when I was seven had a long banana seat and the bar between the legs swooped down to accommodate a dress. The handlebars were curved inward and adorned with tassels. I liked the bike and didn't notice that it was not intended for a little boy, but the older kid across the street and all his skater friends were not so open-minded. They teased me to no end. I removed the tassels, but that didn't fool anyone. Once I couldn't make the whole length of my block without some kid questioning my boyhood, I broke down and told my parents. They replaced the bike with a BMX dirt bike, but as much as I liked the new bike, I always felt a certain kinship with that first one, which sat unused in the garage.

Meanwhile, my sister brought me up listening to Madonna, and I'm talking early mideighties, girl-pop Madonna. She recruited me to be a dancer for the routines she choreographed. I was so desperate to spend time with her that I agreed, and enjoyed it. We spent a whole weekend practicing an intricately elaborate dance performance that encompassed the entire family room and involved chairs and a lot of hands on hips. When our dance routine was perfect, we called our parents down to the living room and performed it for them. They didn't even blink an eye seeing their son strutting the carpet proclaiming he was a material girl. My father applauded when it was over and didn't immediately grab me and insist—as I imagine many fathers would—that the two of us play a game of catch in the backyard or build some stuff with nails. He just rolled with it.

"You're a heterosexual man, right?" I was asked recently at a dinner party. I was asked by a man, someone I'd met recently but who was quickly becoming a friend. I had been in another conversation so the subject caught me off guard. He knew I was involved with a woman, who was sitting across the table from me, so the question was obviously a rhetorical one, but a few different answers ran through my head.

Freud spoke of a "constitutional bisexuality" that begins with one's sexual impulse toward his mother *and* father during the Oedipal days. I could have brought that up. I could have also asked him whether past experiences counted, one of the factors in finding your place on Kinsey's famous scale. If so, I'd have to reacquaint myself with the other factors and get back to him with the appropriate number between zero and six. But in the end I went with "yes," using a leering straight guy tone of voice to subtly mock the question.

"Do you appreciate shoes?" the woman across from him asked. It was clear I was being used to prove some point. Again in my frat-boy voice I said, "Hell yeah, high heels are *hot*. But as far as shoe style and fashion, I couldn't really care." The man nodded, point proven.

I hadn't lied exactly, but I'd certainly misrepresented myself—I had even been known to compliment someone on the choice of footwear. After all my parents had done to make me comfortable with a healthy feminine side—something Jung thought was the key to a whole, healthy psyche—I was trying my damnedest to undermine it. Sometimes, I guess I still felt like that little boy being picked on for riding a girl's bike.

During that summer when I was still pining for Sarah, my mother's *be the vagina* advice wasn't the only anima lesson. One night, Peter explained to me what he thinks happens when a man watches a gorgeous woman walking down the street. Like Jung, he felt that the gaze was projecting something onto her. In Peter's opinion, projecting that desire onto every woman you passed—a bit of a problem for him, he admitted—could be quite weakening. It left him constantly distracted and never feeling centered in his own body.

"The best way to not get defeated by the attraction is to realize that that sexual power exists within you. If you start strutting around like the woman you're looking at—being sexy instead of projecting it onto her—you'll see what I mean."

A couple weeks after Sarah had ended things with me I was taking a walk at night on the main boulevard of Montreal when I remembered Peter's advice. I decided to have a little fun with it and try it, literally. First step was to find a woman I was attracted to. The women in Montreal—who put on high heels and black short skirts to pick up takeout—made that pretty easy. I spotted a gorgeous woman walking on the other side of the street, away from me. She had an insistent stride, but her heels also repeatedly halted her momentum so that her hips jolted side to side with every step. Peter was right, I felt weak just looking at her, hypnotized by the motion, all my energy being sapped by desire. Next step was to imitate her. There wasn't anybody walking right next to me, so I thought what the hell. I swiveled and thrusted my hips. For some reason it didn't feel right to do this if I wasn't also dramatically jutting my shoulders up at the same time. I chuckled to myself, thinking I must look like a vastly uncoordinated runway model. Yeah, *this* is going to get me laid, I thought. A few people glanced at me as I walked by and then glanced away quickly. I ducked into the supermarket to get some smokes.

A couple nights later, I headed over to Heather's apartment, where she and her roommates were having a party. The place was already packed when I got there. I said hello to everyone, chatted with various people, circulated with a beer in my hand. During the whole night, Heather and I circled around each other, first from opposite sides of the perimeter and then closer and closer, swirling like a two-person hurricane until we finally met in the eye. We found a quiet spot on the balcony that overlooked St. Laurent and shared a smoke. We were both very drunk and it was hard to sit up straight so we leaned into each other.

"Right over there," I said, pointing to the main drag, "I went out strutting my inner woman."

"Oh, and how was that for you?"

"I felt pretty sexy, let me tell you."

"You have to do it for me!"

I stood up, pouted my lips, and walked the balcony, vamping it up even more than I had before. She laughed an open-mouth laugh. I liked to make her laugh like that. I laughed at me too. We shoved ourselves closer and kissed.

Not that night, but one night, a week or so later, I discovered an all-important and literal meaning of the word *deep*. Jung had saved me, though once again not exactly in the way my mother had intended.

5

Relationship

(Synchronicity and the Meaning of Love)

I was taking a nap in my dorm room, my face pressed against the pages of an open anthology of American literature, when the phone rang and woke me. Based on the pattern of the ring, I knew another student living in residence was calling me.

"Hello?"

"Hi there," a female voice said. "You don't know me—at least I think you don't know me—but I'm playing a trivia game with friends and I need to come up with the names of the five Jacksons."

"How'd you get my number?"

"I dialed it randomly. Hope you don't mind."

I wiped the drool, which had collected while sleeping, off the side of my face.

"The five Jacksons. You can't do that? That's easy."

"Oh really?"

"Michael, Jermaine . . . and uh, Janet?"

"No, Janet doesn't count."

"Janet should count!"

"I know! But she wasn't part of the Jackson Five. I need the names of the boys."

"Well then, I can only give you two."

"I," she said, pausing for effect, "was able to get four. Michael, Jermaine, Tito, and Marlon. I can't remember the last one."

"Jesse?"

She laughed at that.

Neither of us having any idea who the fifth Jackson was, we abandoned the topic and chatted about various other things including our love of 1980s teen movies, the ridiculously cold weather in Montreal, and psycho-sociological theories that might explain why the other person she called randomly before me did not engage her in conversation as I did. The call lasted for half an hour at least, by the end of which the friends she was playing the game with had given up waiting and had left the room.

"Well, I guess I better go find them," she said finally. We exchanged names and awkwardly left it at that. This was my first encounter with Beth.

Each day when I walked to class and passed the residence building where Beth had told me she was calling from, I looked up and wondered which window was hers. Maybe we were meant to be together, I thought. Later, she told me that she used to look out her window and wonder which guy walking by was me.

My father first explained Jung's concept of synchronicity to me when I was a kid and the two of us were shooting hoops in the driveway. He was listening to his Walkman cassette player as we played, which was unusual.

"Why are you listening to your Walkman?" I asked him as he air-balled a hook shot.

He hit stop. "What?"

"Why are you listening to that?" He recovered the ball and passed it to me.

"Synchronicity," he said. I hit a jumper and asked him what that was. He explained that earlier in the week, he and my mother had been doing their weekly cutting of food coupons out of the newspaper and he had put on an album that he'd recently bought by The Talking Heads. He couldn't explain why but as he listened to it, he noticed the music resonated with him. It fired up something in his unconscious, he told me. So he decided right then to go out and get more of their albums, to listen to some of their older stuff.

This type of spontaneous obsessive behavior from my parents was familiar. Following the Tao—as they liked to do—meant suddenly getting into something because it had arrived into your life for a *reason*. You had to submerge yourself in it as soon as possible to properly remain in the Tao. And remaining in the Tao—which my parents told me was the ancient Chinese name for your "true life path"—was one of the crucial directives of their existence.

After shopping for groceries, my father stopped at the mall, but the music store there carried only the new album, the one he already had. He went to a few other stores but realized that he was going to have to go all the way to the city to find more Talking Heads albums. He knew they'd be there, but he wanted to listen to the music *now*. He felt very strongly about it, he told me, and he was disappointed. Then, just as he was returning home from his failed excursion, pulling into the very driveway where we were playing basketball, the deejay on the radio station he was listening to announced he was about to start a marathon retrospective of the Talking Heads' entire oeuvre. My father ran inside, threw a cassette tape into the stereo and recorded the whole program.

This, he said, was synchronicity. It was a Jungian concept like déjà vu, but unlike déjà vu, where something is familiar but the connection is not known, with synchronicity visible patterns emerge, a string of events and thoughts fall into line. He had followed his Tao and the outside world had responded.

After he explained this to me, my father put his earphones back on and we kept shooting. He was barefoot and so absorbed in the music that he didn't notice that he'd stepped on a piece of glass as we were playing. His foot was bleeding quite a lot by the time he finally felt something "weird," noticed the gash and went inside to clean it up. Sometimes, I learned, following the Tao also meant being a total space cadet.

I walked over to the crack in the driveway that was our free throw line. I was excited by this idea that things happened for a reason, that what happened in the outside world could sometimes magically align with what you were thinking about. I took a shot.

. . .

A year after Beth had randomly called me, one of my roommates was in a play with her. When my friend told Beth the names of the people she was living with, Beth recognized mine. Not long after that, we were introduced during a random run-in at a bookstore. Neither of us said much, intimidated by the sudden pressure of meeting the person that fate had decided we were meant to be with. I couldn't discern much of her body, hidden as it was by a grunge-era button-down shirt and I was thrown off by the fact that she had recently shaved her head and had dyed green the bit of turf that had grown back. After a little small talk in front of the poetry section, we said nice to meet you and went our separate ways.

But then we ran into each other in the grocery store in another part of town, fondling grapefruits. We ran into each other at a concert, sweaty and dancing at the front of the stage. These chance encounters happened a few more times, each in a new location until finally, three years after that first random phone call and three months before I would graduate and leave the city forever, I was visiting the former roommate who had first introduced Beth and me and there was Beth standing in the doorway when I arrived. She was my old roommate's new roommate and, now with short black hair framing her gorgeous smile and wearing a tight tank top splattered in paint, was a lot curvier and sexier than I'd remembered. Something finally clicked. It was love at first, er, sixth sight.

W hen I was in high school, my mother and Peter were both rereading *The Unbearable Lightness of Being* and when they were done with their copy they suggested I read it. One of the characters, Tereza, decides to leave her job as a waitress in a small village to follow the man she has fallen in love with, Tomas, to Prague. The author Milan Kundera interrupts the narrative to explain that the reason the two get together is a string of meaningful coincidences that involve the number six, a song by Beethoven, and the two characters running into each other twice at the same yellow bench. The copy of the book I was reading was filled with notes back and forth between my mother and Peter and during these parts they reminded each other of the synchronicities that had brought them together. At that time, I had come to view their relationship as the ideal and so it was as if they had shared, in the margins of the book, their blueprint for the necessary foundations of love.

Not that the story was without conflict. The book is also about the challenges of fidelity. At the beginning of the book, Tomas is a divorcee who is determined to not get into another emotionally intimate relationship with a woman. Thus, he resolves to live by what he calls the rule of threes. "Either you see a woman three times in quick succession and then never again," Tomas explains in the book, "or you maintain relations over the years but make sure that the rendezvous are at least three weeks apart."

Like my parents, Peter was inclined to the extreme honesty and spontaneous confession that is a side effect of being involved in psychological circles, so I heard about the ongoing affairs that he'd had during his previous marriage. Peter's notes in *The Unbearable Lightness of Being* express some sympathies for Tomas's interest in other women, as well as his affairs, which my mother answered by using evidence from the text to show how Tomas was simply hurting himself—and being unfaithful to his anima—by cheating on Tereza. As far as I know, my mother won that debate.

I'd been in love with women before, but the thing I had with Beth was different. When Heather and I broke up she told me I was afraid of conflict and that I ran at the first sign of trouble, an analysis that stuck with me. With Beth, I decided to stick it out during some of the early rough times, which mostly involved her guilt over breaking up with her previous boyfriend, who was maybe the person leaving anonymous notes at her door, and whom she continued to see on occasion. I stayed, and we worked it out.

One of my first hunches that we might have something good going was that when I fantasized about Beth, she did not dissolve into a cloud of black mist. And although I was attracted to her, I didn't think of her as a black widow spider. I didn't think of her as a dog either, mind you, but she was loyal and affectionate.

A month or so after Beth and I had started seeing each other, we were sitting on a bench in Montreal and I was trying to explain to her that what was happening between us was no longer under our control. I was studying Marlowe and Shakespeare at the time, so it was your typical carpe diem–type monologue, but I was having a hard time finding the right metaphor. Just then, a huge gust of wind came and blew leaves over us. We closed our eyes and squeezed hands until the mini-tornado had passed.

"Our love is like the fall wind," I said, "spiraling leaves across the city." My inner poetess was making it happen.

She kissed me and smiled, but it quickly turned into a frown.

"I'm worried about him," Beth said. She was talking about her ex again.

"Don't worry," I reminded her and searched for another metaphor. And just then a hulking bulldozer pulled up in front of us and flipped open a manhole cover. "Anyway, we have no choice in the matter. Our love is like a bulldozer, tossing a manhole cover aside like it's just a dead leaf thrown across the city in a fall wind."

I wasn't saying these things just to get laid. *Finally*, with Beth that had happened early on and without difficulty. I really did feel that there was some universal force bringing us together.

The leaves blew over us just as I was looking for a metaphor for the power of our draw to each other and then the bulldozer appeared just when I was looking for another. Everywhere Beth and I went, we saw businesses called B&M Carborators or M&B Diner. It was synchronicity! The universe was sending me a message that I was supposed to be with her. That, and I was wearing some serious love goggles.

My father had inculcated me into a belief in synchronicity, but since I have a tendency to be somewhat suggestible—someone who loves me once kindly referred to this quality as "open-minded"—I decided that I should look into the concept from its source and judge for myself. I went to Jung.

Though it was something he often didn't share openly—he had discovered early on in medical school that people raised their eyebrows and began questioning his sanity every time he brought it up—Jung writes in his memoir that even at the beginning of his career he had an interest in supernatural activity and the occult.

His interest originates from two experiences in his family home. Once, home during the summer from university, Jung was studying, and his mother was knitting in a nearby room. "Suddenly there sounded a report like a pistol shot," Jung writes. He rushed into the dining room from where the sound had come and both he and his mother saw that the seventy-year-old walnut table had inexplicably split down the center.

Two weeks later, another loud sound interrupted the household. Jung was away, but when he came home, he was told about it and upon investigation, found that a steel knife in a sideboard had split into many pieces. "A few weeks later," Jung writes, "I heard of certain relatives who had been engaged for some time in table-turning, and also had a medium, a young girl of fifteen and a half." (Table-turning, for those not in supernaturally inclined social spheres, is another word for "séance.") Jung wondered if these activities, which were practiced inside the house itself, were causing the paranormal events. However, because he liked to think of himself as a bona fide scientist, Jung wanted to collect data to prove the theories. So of course, he began attending the séances. He later wrote his dissertation—"On the Psychology and Pathology of So-Called Occult Phenomena"— based on the experiences. But as much as he tried to keep a skeptical point of view, Jung truly started to believe that this young teenage girl—Helly, his cousin—was able to channel spirits. He got sucked into the metaphysical world and he came to believe in the supernatural. This was something that upset his dear colleague Freud.

Many years after the walnut-table incident, Jung was over at Freud's house and Freud gave him an earful about his "nonsensical" occultist beliefs. As Freud lectured him, Jung says he felt "as if my diaphragm were made of iron and were becoming red-hot— a glowing vault." Then, Freud's monologue was suddenly interrupted by such a loud noise from the bookshelf next to them that they both feared it was going to topple.

"There, that is an example of a so-called catalytic exteriorization phenomenon," Jung said to Freud, which was his version of "I told you so." Freud called it "sheer bosh," to which Jung responded by daring the sound to happen again: "You are mistaken, Herr Professor," Jung said. "And to prove my point I now predict that in a moment there will be another such loud report!"

And then indeed, the sound occurred again.

According to Jung, "Freud only stared aghast" at him and then the subject was dropped. Freud did follow up with a letter, though, in which he again asserted that a belief in ghosts and moving furniture could not be taken seriously. Also, he addressed the bookshelf noise. "At first I was inclined to accept this as proof, if the sound that was so frequent while you were here were not heard again after your departure—but since then I have heard it repeatedly, not, however, in connection with my thoughts and never when I am thinking about you or this particular problem of yours. (And not at the present moment, I add by way of a challenge.)" *Zing!*

. . .

Jung dismissed Freud's worries and began investigating supernatural occurrences on the side. When he was seventy-seven, he
published a short text called *Synchronicity: An Acausal Connecting
Principle.*

Synchronicity, he summarizes in the book, "means the simul-
taneous occurrence of a certain psychic state with one or more
external events which appear as meaningful parallels to the
momentary subjective state—and, in certain cases, vice versa."

One example he gives is the story of a late-nineteenth-century
French astronomer named Flammarion, who, while writing a
book about the atmosphere "was just at the chapter on wind-force
when a sudden gust of wind swept all his papers off the table and
blew them out of the window."

Jung then gives his own example related to writing. He was
researching fish symbols in history when he experienced an unusual
confluence of fishiness: he had fish for lunch; later in the day someone made a mention of making an "April fish" of someone; he came
across a transcription that read "Est homo totus medius piscis ab
imo" (he doesn't give a translation of the Latin, but I'll take Jung's
word for it that it involves fish); a former patient brought by some
paintings of fish that she had done; that evening, he was shown "a
piece of embroidery with fish-like sea-monsters in it"; and the next
morning, a patient came in and told Jung a dream in which "she
stood on the shore of a lake and saw a large fish that swam straight
towards her and landed at her feet." A few months later, Jung had
just finished writing about this series of fish events and was taking
a break when he encountered "a fish a foot long" lying on top of a

seawall near his summer home. "Since no one else was present, I have no idea how the fish could have got there," he wrote.

Several years ago, when I was doing initial research for this book, I was having dinner with Beth and she asked me to define synchronicity. I tried out a few explanations, but I wasn't sure I'd quite nailed it. Then, the next day, I got an e-mail from her with the subject line, "synchronicity!" Beth was at work and an author had delivered to her the rough draft of a book. As she was skimming through the pages, she noticed there was one sticky note poking out of the side. She flipped to that page to see what it might be highlighting, but it appeared to be placed there randomly. However, upon scanning the text next to it, she came across a sidebar defining synchronicity. A synchronicity involving synchronicity. Metasynchronicity! I win.

(Dare I even mention that as I write these very words, *Sleepless in Seattle* is playing on my television, a film based on synchronicity?)

In his book on synchronicity, Jung shares a story that he got from another writer, someone who collected anecdotes about lost objects miraculously finding their way back to their owners. In one, a woman takes pictures of her son and drops the roll of film off to be developed. War breaks out and she can't manage to pick up the film before she has to flee the country. Two years later and back home, she buys a roll of film, takes pictures of her new daughter and when she picks up the developed photos, she finds that the images of her daughter are double-exposed over the old shots of her son. She concludes that the film, never developed, amazingly made its way back into circulation on the shelves where she purchased it once again.

The story does sound amazing, but Jung doesn't discuss the possibility that, in the chaos and distress of wartime, the woman just misremembered dropping off the roll. Then later, perhaps she double-exposed the same one she thought she dropped off. It could have been as simple as that. This isn't to say, though, that things don't sometimes happen that have very low odds.

The Argentinean writer Jorge Luis Borges wrote a story about a fictional—and impossible—library that contained all the possible books that could ever exist. In this library, every possible variation of letters and spaces was represented by one of the books in the collection. As such, the vast majority of the books were complete gibberish. But, since every permutation of alphabetical ordering had one instance in the library, there also existed in it every work by Dostoevsky, a copy of whatever is currently number one on the *New York Times* bestseller list, as well as masterpieces and bombs that have yet to be written. I would suggest that when you take into account that six billion people on the planet are experiencing hundreds—countless, really—of new events per day, it is conceivable that eventually, *everything* will happen.

At some point, a man will flip a coin fifty times and it will land heads up all fifty times. This will likely only happen once, but to the individual who witnesses it, it will feel magical because essentially he has won the fate lottery. But how much meaning should we ascribe to these occurrences?

Regardless, they make the best stories.

. . .

When Jacob and I were getting together, synchronicities were happening all over the place. The *j* on my typewriter starting to work again the night we first hooked up was the first example. But then, we'd see our initials together everywhere just as I later did with Beth. One time, Jacob and I were driving around Denver and talking about the university that we both wanted to get into and go to together and right then, a delivery truck for a company with the same name passed by.

I always felt when synchronicities were happening to me that it meant things were on the right course in my life and they tended to happen a lot when I was in love. And in love, I guess I wanted to see the connections everywhere. They became enfolded into the story. Of course, the synchronicities did always tend to fade after a while, the Jungian version of settling into a real relationship. At some point with Beth, I stopped seeing everything as a sign of our undying love for each other and, in fact, sometimes the signs seemed to point in the opposite direction. Well, I suppose every good love story needs an obstacle to overcome.

———————————

One night after we'd been living in New York for about a year, Beth and I went to see a play with some friends. Nadia, to whom we'd been recently introduced, was going to be there. The theater entrance was also a small art gallery and when we arrived, she was already there, standing in front of a painting. I hung back while everyone said hello to her and then started wandering around to look at the art. Nadia was beautiful but not in a typical way. She had sharp features that gave her a naturally intense expression. She was very small in stature but seemed to command everyone's attention simply by will of her excellent posture. I tried to ignore her for a while but the more I did the more I could only think about where she was. And then finally, when Beth was at the other side of the gallery, I approached.

"Hello," I said. I considered the painting she was looking at. It was red.

"Hi, Micah. What do you think?"

"It's intense. Makes me think of blood."

She nodded slowly. So far, this had been the most extensive one-on-one conversation that we'd had.

"And what do you think?" I asked.

"You know, it doesn't really say anything to me."

Then we were swept up by Beth and our friends to be seated for the play, and I was stuck wondering whether her comment on the painting was a Jungian-style projection of the way she felt about me. Was her unconscious saying that she thought I had nothing to say? Maybe she was even consciously trying to communicate that to me. Or was it perhaps that it was I who was projecting my own insecurity onto her and she wasn't even thinking about me? That was also possible. I couldn't decide which projection equation was the most upsetting. As we walked into the theater, my mind considered another ten variations until, like trying to see the last of your reflections in two facing mirrors, arcing off into infinity, my psyche collapsed in exhaustion and gave up.

I tried to seat myself so that I was far away from Nadia, but in last-minute musical chairs, I ended up next to her. She was on my right, sitting cross-legged in her chair, making herself comfortable. To my left was Beth, holding my hand. I remember very little of the drama on stage.

I had certainly been attracted to other women before, but usually on the subway or walking down the street, moments that passed easily without my having to wrestle with them. If it happened at a party or a bar I just avoided becoming overly flirtatious or would even just ignore the person altogether. I could not avoid Nadia though, or if there had been a chance to avoid becoming drawn in by her, then I had missed it. After a while, I didn't want to avoid her. In fact, I started to wonder if I was supposed to be with her instead of Beth.

Then one night out at a bar, Nadia was again sitting to my right, on a barstool. We were chatting about something I can't remember now when she leaned close and told me, "Ever since the day I first saw you, I had a crush on you." It seemed pretty gutsy considering Beth was once again sitting to my left, talking to someone else.

"Me too," I said, but then changed the subject quickly. She didn't push it, just sort of smirked and left it at that. I eventually excused myself to the bathroom and then avoided Nadia for the rest of the night. I was relieved when it was finally time to go home. On our way to the subway, I put my arm around Beth.

"You're attracted to Nadia, aren't you?" she said.

My mind fired off into a million directions trying to decide how I was going to handle this. I decided to go with a lie.

"Well, not really. I mean, sure, I can see that objectively she's an attractive person, but I'm not necessarily attracted *to her.*"

"Micah, it's okay. You can just tell me if you're attracted to her."

"Okay, I guess I am attracted to her. Sorry."

She was silent for a minute, during which my mind again went through its calculations to decide whether there would ever be a way out the mess I'd just gotten myself into.

"But she's nothing compared to you," I said. "I mean, she's good-looking but sort of awkwardly angular in this—"

"I have a little bit of a crush on her too," Beth said, interrupting my bumbling.

"Oh?" I hadn't expected that. "Okay. That's good I guess."

But then suddenly I realized I was now faced with a problem more complicated than my having a crush on someone else—*both* Beth and I having a crush on someone else. Beth's crushes were something I didn't have any control over.

"She told me that she was attracted to me," Beth said, blushing.

"What? She just told me that same thing!"

"She's playing both of us," Beth said, laughing.

We reached our front door, and before walking in, I stopped and put my hands gently on Beth's shoulders. "I think I know how to handle this."

When I was a teenager, my mother started talking about sending me to a Process Work seminar like the ones I had witnessed when I was a kid. It was never on the top of my list of things to do in the summer, but since I'd been around Process Work most of my life, I was curious what it would be like. Plus, my mother kept insisting: "It'll be amazing! You'll learn so much about yourself!"

During my last summer break before graduating from university, my mother told me a good one was coming to town. Arny wasn't going to be leading it, but one of his star pupils would be, with assistance from her partner. I said sure and my mother signed me up.

The seminar took place at a communal housing complex in the suburbs of Denver, a liberal oasis in the middle of the Republican wilds of Colorado. I imagined that surrounding us for hundreds of miles were families of gun-toting rednecks, and meanwhile we at the seminar would be getting ready to follow the unconscious messages sent to us through our tics and sneezes.

The first day, we learned how to walk. Or rather, we were instructed to discover our "true gait." If you really paid attention, the facilitator told us, there was a tiny *feeling* of wanting to walk another way than one normally did, the way society tells us to walk. You might notice, for instance, that your right foot was dragging just a tiny bit. After we'd noticed that sort of irregularity, we were to emphasize it, drag it even more, *really* drag it until it is a just a dead leg and your other foot is hopping to keep your body moving. That would be an example of a true gait.

Mine, as it turns out, was to be bent over backward like I was walking into a very powerful wind. Or, alternatively, I could have been doing the limbo. I've tried to do this walk again every

now and then and have found it's really good for working out my
hamstrings, but basically, this exercise taught me nothing. On
the second day of the seminar, however, I learned how to perform under a far more challenging type of being in limbo. That is,
how to preserve a monogamous relationship in the face of outside
attraction.

"Today," our instructor announced when we had all arrived and
quieted down, "we're going to look at how to integrate third-
person energy into a relationship."

She paused and thoughtfully looked at each and every person
in the room. The silent gaze was something I remembered Arny
doing when I was a kid.

"What do we do when one person in a couple develops an
attraction to a person outside the relationship?"

"Threesome?" someone said. Most of the room laughed. I figured a good number of the people in that predominantly purple-
attired room had experienced at least one threesome in their lives,
if not a foursome or fivesome. Was it the failed hippie revolution
that had led to the rise of alternative therapies? I wondered this
as I imagined having a threesome with the teacher and her partner. I was mostly just attracted to the partner. She was slim and
composed, had slender fingers, long legs, and wide lips. In fact,
everything about her was elongated, like the depiction of aliens
in movies. Not being green, however, she was far better looking.
I realized, though, that our threesome would fail as many often
did, because I was not attracted enough to the teacher and so
there would be an inequality. I would just want to be getting her

out of the way the entire time. Maybe I could just have a secret rendezvous with the partner?

"You," the teacher said, pointing to one of the group, "come up here." The woman she pointed to stood next to her. "Let's say I'm attracted to you. We're flirting at a party." At this point, the teacher saucily walked up to the woman she picked. "Hiya, how ya doin'?" She leered down the woman's shirt.

The woman offered a shy "hello."

"Hey, what's going on here?" her hot partner said, busting in all upset.

The teacher turned to the class. "Okay, so now we have a third-person attraction coming in between us, the couple," she said, pointing to herself and her partner. She told the third person she could sit down.

"I'm attracted to her," she said to her partner.

"Why? Am I not enough for you?"

"Well, she's kind of shy. I find it cute."

"Oh really?" Her partner made a melodramatic frown and tightened her fists in a cartoonlike display of anger.

The teacher turned to the class. "Now I need to think a bit more deeply about what it is exactly that I like about this third person. Why do I like that she's shy? Instead of me answering that question, can anyone here tell me why I might be attracted to her shyness?"

The class, obviously filled with insecure, shy people, was silent.

"Maybe it's an expression of vulnerability," the teacher said. She turned back to her partner. "I like that she expresses her vulnerability, her fears. She blushes when she's nervous. She wears her nerves on her skin."

"So you want me to be more vulnerable?"

"Or maybe *I* need to be more like that," she answered, raising her eyebrows and turning to the class with a meaningful look in her eye, once again going around the room gazing at each one of us.

It was kind of an aha! moment for me. Previously, I always thought the key to love was to just keep searching for the person who did everything the way you wanted and brought into your life all of the things that you didn't possess. The teacher explained that it was not simply up to her partner to change and be more like the person she had a crush on. That could be part of it, she said, but even more important was that she—the person who had the crush in the first place—figured out a way to bring into the relationship what the crush symbolized. She herself needed to be more vulnerable. Like Peter's embodying the sexiness of the women walking down the street in order to retain the power of his sexuality, you could embody an attraction to a third person to reinforce the monogamous relationship.

There is a great irony, of course, in using post-Jungian practices to maintain a monogamous relationship. My parents had failed to remain in a healthy, happy marriage, but I figured that was because they were just minor psychologists. As I began reading about Jung's life to gain insight into the ideas around which I was raised, I had assumed I would be given the picture of psychological and marital perfection. As it turns out, Jung was human—and not monogamous at all. In fact, he was decidedly *un*monogamous. Forget about his reputed affairs; for a decade, Jung kept a mistress whom he brought out in public and who was for all intents and purposes recognized by the psychological community as a second wife.

Jung fell in love with Emma, the woman who would become his wife—the official one—when he was twenty-four and she was seventeen. The two carried on a long-distance correspondence through letters, during which they began what would become an intellectual, as well as romantic, relationship. Emma had wanted to go away to university but was forbidden by her father to do so; she was drawn to Jung's support of her intellectual pursuits and although he was from a lower class and she knew she'd be supporting him, in the end, she accepted his proposal of marriage.

Though it may not hold up in a court of law, some anecdotal evidence of Jung's affairs exists, including the claim made by Sabina Spielrein. In one of his letters to Freud during the Spielrein period, Jung addressed how his feelings for her had enlightened him about his personal problem remaining faithful. "Meanwhile I have learnt an unspeakable amount of marital wisdom, for until now I had a totally inadequate idea of my polygamous components despite all self-analysis. Now I know where and how the devil can be laid by the heels. These painful yet extremely salutary insights have churned me up hellishly inside, but for that very reason, I hope, have secured me moral qualities which will be of the greatest advantage to me in later life." So it seems Jung was optimistic he had enough awareness of his wandering eye to control it. Ultimately, however, that was not to be the case.

As soon as he'd successfully navigated the Spielrein debacle, into his office strolled Toni Wolff. Wolff was a young woman of twenty-one when she became Jung's client, but she quickly became his intellectual partner, and then finally his long-term lover. Every day, before lunch, she would arrive at Jung's house and the two would sit in his office and talk about psychology or analyze each other. Wolff helped Jung refine his ideas and is even credited with originating some of them. Although Emma was embarrassed and jealous, she decided in the end to allow the relationship to continue without making a public fuss. The three of them would go out with Emma on one of Jung's arms and Toni on the other. Everyone in the scene knew about the triangle, but it was never spoken of directly.

In an interview with biographer Deirdre Bair after Jung's death, Jung's son Franz rhetorically expressed the anguish that Emma must have felt: "Can you imagine living with a man who left you with full responsibility for his house and his children while he passed the time playing their games or being in that same house with another woman?"

Jung did finally address his long-term infidelity in early versions of his memoir: "What could you expect from me?—the anima bit me on the forehead and would not let go."

"What is it that attracts you to Nadia?" I asked Beth in that fluffy-edged psychologist voice that my father often used when talking to clients, or my sister. We were back at our apartment.

"Micah, do you really want me to answer that?"

"Yes, it's okay, we're doing a process."

Beth knew what this meant, but had never been involved in one herself.

"I'm not sure that's a good idea."

"I think this will work."

"You're not a psychologist, Micah."

I sighed.

"She's confident," Beth said.

"Yes, she is that," I replied. "Not to mention devious."

"She takes risks, you know."

"Okay, I agree. You can stop there." I squinted my eyes and grew silent, tried out the slow nodding. "So based on this, the process is telling us that we both have crushes on Nadia because we are trying to bring more risk into our relationship."

"And not because we both think she's hot?" Beth said, suppressing a laugh.

"Good," I said. "See, that was a risky joke. You could have hurt my feelings by challenging my psychoanalytic authority."

"Confidence *is* kind of hot," Beth said.

We spent the next hour deconstructing our attraction for Nadia and realized that we'd slipped into a lull in our relationship where we weren't trying out new things or telling each other enough what we wanted from each other or for ourselves. It ended up seeming less like a Jungian transformative experience and more like the kind of discussion *Cosmo* magazine is always telling couples to have.

I think more than anything, the fact that we were bonding over picking apart Nadia brought us back together again.

Anyway, although Beth never let me play psychologist with her again, it seemed to have worked. My attraction to Nadia faded.

Jacob was always intrigued to hear my Jungian solutions to life's problems, but when I told him about the "Nadia process," he echoed the same comment I'd heard years before in the seminar.

"Why didn't you just have a threesome?" he asked. Unlike the person who blurted this out at the commune, he meant it seriously. When Jacob and I were together in high school, we'd had several of them. The odd one was fun, but I found it more stressful than anything.

"Monogamy just sets up a relationship for failure," Jacob proclaimed. "I mean, look at all the divorces and cheating. It's unrealistic. People should just let themselves have open relationships."

"The idea of an open relationship makes me want to vomit," I replied. "I like monogamy because it's like a circle—a ring—that the couple is enclosed in and they build up energy between them and they're safe."

"Sure, safe like zoo animals in a cage."

Later, I came across a story about Jung's polygamous lifestyle that expresses well my feelings on it. According to an account from one of Jung's friends mentioned in Deirdre Bair's biography, Jung at least once considered suicide during the years he was involved with Toni Wolff: "His confusion about how to ensure that each woman received the same degree of respect and that they were treated equally was so overwhelming that one day while swimming in the lake, he thought the only solution was to stop trying to stay afloat and let himself drown."

One wife is definitely enough for me.

A few weeks after our pseudo-therapy session, Beth and I had Nadia over for brunch. We'd decided that there was no reason we should not remain friends with her simply because she had tempted both of us and tried to turn our lives into an insidious game of dangerous liaisons. I wonder now if we were—unconsciously, of course—considering a threesome.

I cooked us fried egg sandwiches and we all sat in the living room eating quietly. Nadia wasn't saying anything and it occurred to me for the first time that her silence—which I had previously thought of as a sign of power—might just be a sign that she was as socially awkward as the rest of us.

Jung went to great lengths to prove scientifically that things which occur outside of the psyche can have a meaningful and acausal connection with the psyche. Unfortunately, he chose to prove this by studying the correspondence of love relationships—marriage, actually—to astrology, both of them questionable enterprises. Jung gathered birth dates for the husbands and wives in 483 marriages and worked out their astrological charts. According to Jung, astrologers had come to the conclusion hundreds of years ago that three specific astrological pairings existed that led most often to a successful marriage. These were not simply two signs—Libra and Gemini, for example—but involved the position of the sun, the moon, as well as other planetary bodies. Jung looked at his 483 couples' charts to see if their combination did indeed correspond to any of these three pairings.

The astrological data came to him in three batches. In the first, one of the "classical" pairings was prominent in the couples, leading Jung to be initially excited that indeed this synchronicity of love and the planetary alignment existed. The second batch, however, highlighted the second pairing, an inconsistancy that concerned Jung. But when the third batch then highlighted the third pairing, he again got excited.

"The chance arrangement of the marriage horoscopes," he wrote, "which were simply piled on top of one another as they came in from the most diverse sources, and the equally fortuitous way they were divided into three unequal batches, suited the sanguine expectations of the research workers and produced an overall picture that could scarcely have been improved upon from the standpoint of the astrological hypothesis."

In other words, the very fact that the scientific study failed to verify anything scientifically and just mirrored what the researchers had been looking for, bolstered Jung's idea of the synchronistic relationship between an observer and the outside world.

After those three batches, the more data Jung considered, the more nonprominent any of the combinations became. This fading of results he attributed to waning interest in the experiment on his own part and that of his researchers. He compared the results to a similar decrease in the extrasensory perception talents of certain subjects during experiments conducted by J. B. Rhine at Duke University in the early 1930s.

Whatever the results, Jung kept enfolding them into his theory. Though I still like to think that things happen for a reason, in the end, maybe this fact illuminates another explanation of synchronicity: pure chance as seen through optimism goggles.

———

I had a dream not long after the Nadia incident. Beth and I were in bed and above us, dancing along the ceiling, were six beautiful, blonde, round-cheeked children, three boys and three girls. Our six spawn were bouncing around with Beth-like vivaciousness and were also floating and drifting with the kind of spaciness that often characterizes me. When I woke up, I looked over at Beth as she slept. I'd always kept a secret file in my head of provisional plans for a future break up. I thought I'd do it before I was twenty-five, which I had naively calculated was on the outside edge of being too old to meet another person to grow old with. That morning, however, I could no longer access that file. Beth looked exactly like the future mother of my children.

6

The Shadow

(My Archetypal Lust for Violence)

"I had this dream last night I was with Sue and the two of us
went to Starbucks. I ordered a chai latte."
"And?"
"And that was it."
"That's boring."
"I know. It's always like that for me. I wish I had nightmares."
—Conversation overheard on subway

One morning several years ago, Beth and I got into a disagreement over something I can't remember. Only, she
didn't know there had been a disagreement because I'd failed to
let her know I disagreed. I'd just listened to her side—which was
completely unjustified, I can assure you—and grown frustrated.
After she left for work, I walked into my office, grabbed the nearest book—the copy of Joseph Campbell's *Primitive Mythology*
that my father had bought me, as it turned out—and launched
it across the entire length of our apartment. After I let go, the
force exerted felt tremendously satisfying, but as the book began
its journey, I became aware that it was on course to hit the liv-

ing room table lamp, the one that Beth had spent weeks, maybe months, shopping for. I cringed as I watched the book spinning and flapping its way perfectly toward the unintended target. I waved my arms like a hopeful field goal kicker trying to influence its trajectory, but to no avail. The book zeroed in on the lamp and struck it, knocking it to the ground.

"Shit," I said aloud. I walked over to the lamp, inspected it, turned it on and off, found that it was in working order and used the dust ring on the small table on which it had been sitting to place it back exactly where it had been before. Maybe she wouldn't even notice, I thought to myself, pleased.

But then my mood changed. I realized, while staring at that lamp back in its place, that Beth would never know that I had been angry. I decided enough was enough. I had been passive aggressive for too long: moving out of people's way on the sidewalk, not telling coworkers that I thought they were wrong, finding ways around arguments. Never expressing anger—one of the most basic emotions—was like trying to write using only four of the five vowels. I obviously possessed anger and *active* aggression, it just only came out when I was alone or with inanimate objects.

Jung had helped me get an erection and I'd leaned on him again to get laid. I figured it should be no problem for him to help me not be a doormat. I considered calling up my parents for direction, but decided in the end to do this one on my own. I figured I had gleaned enough over the years to perform the analysis without them.

I imagined sitting across from my father in his office. "Well, it's pretty obvious, my son," he'd say. "You need to confront the dark side of your unconscious. You need to confront your shadow."

A few years earlier, I'd had a nightmare while visiting my mother. I told it to her over breakfast. In the dream, I was lined up against a wall with some other people and we were being held hostage by a very large man with a shotgun. It seemed that there was nothing I was going to be able to do to stop him from killing us. If I ran he'd shoot me, but if I just stood there I'd be putting off the inevitable. He was going to execute us. I decided to make a move on the small chance that I would be able to overpower him and escape. I was nervous, though, and wasted time building up my resolve. Before I was able to do anything, he turned the barrels toward me and I woke up.

"It sounds like he's your shadow," my mother said when I finished.

I was familiar with the concept—it was one of my favorites in Jung's oeuvre.

"Does the man in the dream remind you of anyone?" she asked.

I thought about it for a minute, but nobody came to mind.

"It doesn't have to be someone you know personally," she added.

I pictured the killer in my head. He was quite tall and had been wearing a long black trench coat and dark sunglasses. His head was bald. Then it suddenly hit me who he was.

"He's Morpheus!" I exclaimed.

"Huh," my mother said. "Isn't Morpheus the guy in *The Matrix* who helps Keanu Reeves wake up to see reality?"

I was deeply impressed—not so much by my mother's unfolding interpretation of my dream, but by her surprising access to contemporary sci-fi pop-culture referents. Still, I had to correct her.

"It's Neo, Mom."

"Right," she said. "Neo, which means 'new'."

"Morpheus is actually a good guy in the film," I informed her, "though Neo doesn't know that at first."

"A part of you wants to wake yourself up to a new reality," she said. "Now is there a way you could be more like Morpheus in your life?"

"I don't think so, Mom. I'm just not that badass."

"What would it mean to you," she asked seriously, "to face a situation with a shotgun?"

As the son of pacifists—my father was a conscientious objector during the war in Vietnam—I didn't know how she expected me to answer that question. But, being the son of Jungians, I knew I was supposed to access the knowledge by tapping into the collective unconscious, which is like an extremely well-stocked Halloween costume shop.

"With certainty?" I said, unsure that that was the right answer.

"Ah ha!" My mother nodded at me knowingly. "Is there something in your life that you could approach with more certainty, more like a badass?" she asked.

Everything, I thought to myself, but how exactly was one supposed to be more certain about something than one was? Again, I wasn't sure.

"If there is a part of me that is as badass as Morpheus," I told her, "then I've never met it."

The concept of the archetype—among which the shadow, along with the anima, is one of the most fundamental examples—is one of Jung's most well-known discoveries and is something he worked on refining his entire life. While reading his memoir, I was entertained to learn that Jung first came to the idea as he was lying to Freud about a dream he'd had.

Back when Jung was still Freud's crown prince, the two took a trip to the United States to plant their seeds in the New World.

"We were together every day, and analyzed each other's dreams," Jung wrote. "At the time I had a number of important ones, but Freud could make nothing of them."

In one of these dreams, Jung is in a house that he identifies as his own, though it is not the house from his real life. He walks through it, noting that the upper floor is a "salon furnished with fine old pieces in rococo style." Down the stairs from the salon is the ground floor, which he says is much older, decorated in medieval furnishings. The cellar has "walls that dated from Roman times" and then a secret door in the floor of the cellar leads down into a cave, where Jung discovers bones and "two human skulls, obviously very old and half disintegrated." Then he woke up.

Freud thought that dreams were enactments of repressed

wishes, so he insisted Jung confess whom he wanted dead. Jung hesitated but, pressed for an answer, he replied that he wanted his wife and sister-in-law to die. (Writing about this encounter much later after his wife had already passed away, Jung assures readers that he did not really want his wife and sister-in-law dead; he just wanted Freud to get the interpretation over with.)

Jung felt he already knew what the dream meant, but he didn't want to upset his mentor by telling him this. "I did not feel up to quarrelling with him, and also I feared that I might lose his friendship if I insisted on my point of view."

The night before, Jung had been thinking about Freud's theories, once again wondering if his mentor's habit of viewing everything that happened in the unconscious through the lens of sexuality was too narrow.

"My dream was giving me the answer," wrote Jung. He decided the historical layers of his dream were a sign that there existed ancient imprints on his psyche that had nothing to do with fondling himself as a child. Just as the anima was an empty container into which we placed personal preferences relating to women, there were hundreds of other forms as well—the hero, the villain, the joker, the husband, the wife, etc.—that were created collectively and passed down through generations.

"It was my first inkling of a collective a priori beneath the personal psyche," Jung wrote. "This I first took to be the traces of earlier modes of functioning. Later, with increasing experience and on the basis of more reliable knowledge, I recognized them as forms of instincts, that is, as archetypes."

Jung suggests this is why the same type of characters and stories have appeared throughout human history even if no contact has been made between cultures. The shadow, one of the more generic archetypes, appears simply as The Other to the protagonist: Darth Vader to Luke Skywalker, or Morpheus to me.

Once Jung decided that we all carried these common forms within us, he went mad studying history and mythology to amass the data that would describe them.

When I was fifteen, my father had part of his Jungian dissertation excerpted in an anthology about the shadow.

"Hey, Micah, come look at this!" he shouted from the kitchen. When I arrived, he was opening a big cardboard box that was sitting on the table. He pulled out a couple copies of the book and handed one to me. He was beaming.

The book was called *Meeting the Shadow: The Hidden Power of the Dark Side of Human Nature.* I turned to the table of contents and saw his name, which came right after Joseph Campbell's, one of his heroes. I was impressed—this was by far the coolest thing my father had ever done.

He told me that he had written the text quite a long time ago, when I was a boy. I laughed, remembering well that period of time when he was in a perpetually bad mood, spending hours and hours reading in his office, seated in the spotlight of a standing lamp in the corner of the room. He'd refuse to come out and play, even when I whined.

I looked up from the book. "Dad, you've turned to the dark side." He grinned and laughed an evil, mischievous laugh.

We discussed the shadow for a while, which was my first in-depth introduction to the concept. He explained to me that the shadow was the name Jung gave to the part of your personality that you disown, all the qualities that you think you do not possess. Jung thought that we actually did possess these qualities and that if we did not accept that fact, we could be dangerously influenced by them. Shadow qualities, he said, were usually negative but some of them were positive as well.

"So the part of me that likes to do the dishes is my shadow?" I interrupted.

"Exactly," my father said laughing. "Also, the part of you that likes to clean the litter box."

I took a copy of *Meeting the Shadow* to my room and read my father's chapter, titled "The Usefulness of the Useless."

The article draws on two Taoist myths to illustrate that things we usually think of as negative can actually be positive. In one of them, a carpenter arrives in a village that possesses an oak tree so enormous that "more than ten of its branches were big enough to be made into boats." But despite this rich bounty, the carpenter just walks on by, barely even glancing at the tree. When the carpenter's assistant asks the carpenter why he doesn't stop and chop it down to use for building, the carpenter replies that the tree's wood is flawed and could make nothing worthwhile and that is why it is so old and enormous. The story, my father writes, illustrates "the importance the Taoists attributed to the seemingly useless—to those things that individuals and society shun due to their lack of utility." Useful trees, he points out, get stripped of their fruits and then chopped down, whereas useless ones are left alone to thrive and grow old.

"One of the major ways to integrate our inner opposites is by consciously confronting the shadow—the 'dark' part of the personality that contains the undesirable qualities and attributes we refuse to 'own,'" my father wrote in his essay. "Facing and owning these attributes is a difficult and painful process, for although the shadow may contain positive elements of personality, it primarily consists of our inferiorities—primitive, unadapted, and awkward aspects of our nature that we have rejected due to moral, aesthetic, and socio-cultural considerations."

I smiled. It takes a special kind of father—a Jungian one—to encourage one's son to be immoral.

My father concluded his article by sending his reader out on a mission, though an admittedly vague one: "In other words, we should aim at becoming ourselves and bring *what we are* into the world."

Freudians and Jungians alike are famous for asking clients to describe their childhoods at length and in great detail. Of course, if I had repressed my inner shotgun-wielding psychopath properly, I shouldn't be able to access him, but there were a couple memories that I thought might give my inner therapist some clue into my dark side. The first—which involved a persona I called Naked Man—occurred when I was seven and enjoying my "auto-erotic" phase.

Naked Man was a superhero. He wore a blue cape like Batman and he launched from his lair to head out on secret missions, though his superhero purpose was not as altruistic as that of, say, Superman. Naked Man's greatest adventure—"The Flight of Naked Man," as it became known—consisted of Naked Man traversing the entirety of the house, from his bedroom on the top floor, through the living room and kitchen, to the family room and then back again, all while being completely and totally, with the exception of the blue cape heroically streaming from his back, naked. Also crucial was that while it was okay for others to be aware of Naked Man's moving presence in the house, no one should ever gain awareness of his nakedness.

What saved Naked Man from the disaster of discovery was that Naked Man's mother—who, unlike the mothers of many superheroes, was still alive—was often very concentrated on cooking or paying bills or whatever it was she was doing and thus did not notice Naked Man's quiet padding, or chose not to acknowledge his quickly passing—and naked—presence.

Naked Man was never caught. He triumphed! There was one close call, however, when Naked Man was, for reasons he can no longer remember, involved in a very different sort of adventure.

On that day, after a successful return to his lair, Naked Man decided to do something with Snow White. Snow White was, to Naked Man, very attractive, though he could not put his finger on exactly why. She was very kind to those little dwarfs, she slept in their bed, and she wore that tight blue shirt that accentuated her chest. In retrospect, perhaps it's not so hard to imagine why Naked Man found Snow White so attractive.

Naked Man didn't know what was supposed to be done with

Snow White. He had heard of sex, but didn't know what it was, what it actually entailed. He knew that the something to be done with Snow White was done in bed, under sheets, privately. It was definitely not something that was supposed to be discovered by, for instance, Naked Man's sister opening the door without knocking.

"Micah, what are you *doing*?"

Panicking!

"Nothing."

Nothing besides realizing that my life was now over.

"Why are you in bed in the middle of the afternoon?"

"I'm taking a nap."

"No you're not."

"I'm just lying down."

Naked Man thought—he desperately hoped—that she would go away at that, but there she stood, unfazed, as if she were going to spend the next ten years of their lives just watching him and judging.

"Are you *masturbating*?"

"No!"

Andreya valued her privacy more than anyone and she could probably sense that she was about to make a major trespass.

"Well, you're doing something under there. I'll leave you to it. Do you want me to close the door?"

"Yes, thank you."

On her way out, she turned around for one last peek.

"Have fun masturbating."

"I'm not masturbating!" I shouted at the door as it closed.

It was true, I was *not* masturbating. I didn't even know exactly what masturbation was. Somehow, though, I sensed Andreya was not far off the mark.

Here's what I was doing: I, as Naked Man, was contemplating stabbing Snow White between the legs with a knife. The thing about the fantasy was I could never complete it in my head. I never actually stabbed Snow White and she never bled. The moment of penetration was inexpressible to my imagination. I knew that there was something wrong, even violent in this action—I was only seven, but not born yesterday—but it was compelling for reasons I could not understand.

My inner therapist nodded and made some notes about the connection between my latent aggression and sexuality. Perhaps Freud was right after all? It's certainly clear that sometimes a knife is *not* just a knife, but actually *is* standing in for something else.

A few years later, I had another "peak" shadow moment while partaking in another secret adventure.

It was winter, and even though technically the garage was still inside, I could see my breath as I entered. I shut the door quietly behind me, a procedure that took a whole minute to do properly so that the click of the lock was rendered nearly silent. My parents weren't home yet—I had just returned from school—but with their odd schedules, I never knew when I would hear my mother's footsteps in the kitchen or when the garage door's bracingly loud motor would suddenly fire up, raising the curving threshold one panel at a time to allow my father to park his Jeep. My sister was home, but she was less of a worry, reliably sedentary in after-school hours—either parked in front of the television to follow the romantic misadventures of Patch and Kayla on *Days of Our Lives*, or in her room with the door closed listening to her stereo at full volume.

Once it was safe, I turned on the light. I put down my secret stash of Ding Dongs on top of one of the cardboard boxes that filled the perimeter of the garage and listened carefully to make sure once again there were no noises coming from the kitchen. Then I proceeded to rip open the silver plastic wrapping and shove the Ding Dongs into my mouth.

For those who have not been fortunate enough to consume one, a Ding Dong is a chocolate-covered, chocolate cupcake with a creamy white center, mass-produced into the shape of a hockey puck. When I was a kid, each box of Ding Dongs came with enough to supply me with two weeks' worth of school lunch desserts. However, unlike my best friend Charlie's mother, mine did not prepare my lunch. I packed it myself and so no one was monitoring my dessert consumption. If I was willing to forego having lunch desserts for two weeks, I could eat all the Ding Dongs in one day. On this particular day, I had taken five.

As the chocolate coating melted, the white cream in the center dissolved instantly into pure sugar-water, injecting itself into the glands at the back of my mouth, firing up the blood in my face, flushing my cheeks. The cakey part expanded, then turned to a thick, viscous chocolate lava, suffocating me as I battled it down my throat. But I did not want to breathe—at all times, I wanted more and more Ding Dong, I wanted to keep eating and never stop. My heart raced and I could see nothing—all my senses were drowned by the deliriousness of my saccharine blood.

From the outside, the whole procedure must have appeared

mechanical: open package, shove into mouth, swallow while opening next package. I acted with military efficiency because I needed to be finished as soon as possible so as to reduce my chance of being caught. However, often when I got to the last one, I would slow down, rationalizing that if I were caught at that point, sneaking one dessert was not so bad.

After I took the first bite of my last Ding Dong, I relaxed and took a look around the garage. In red marker, the box in front of me was labeled "Magazines." My parents had a subscription to *National Geographic*, which usually sat on the coffee table in the living room. I liked looking at the pictures. I pulled at the cardboard flaps and they spiraled open like the secret entrance in a James Bond film.

The cover of the magazine on the top did not show a helicopter view of the pointed peaks of the Alps or the lushly fertile landscape of a Vietnamese rice paddy. Instead it displayed a nude woman, her mountains and valleys completely exposed for all to see. I had just discovered the New World.

At that moment, my mouth and hands covered in chocolate, I was bathing in so much sin that I almost passed out. My heart pounded and I could barely breathe as I turned the cover and flipped through the pages to see more. This was very *bad*, I thought, and I should not be doing this. I turned a couple more pages and saw an extreme close-up of that part of the anatomy that I hadn't seen since, I suppose, my birth. Then I heard a noise, a snap or a click somewhere. I froze, listening to gauge from where the threat would emerge, but I heard nothing else.

I put the magazine back in the box, making sure to set it down exactly as I had found it, folded the box in on itself just as it had been before, and tiptoed into the house, shoving the empty wrappers to the very bottom of the trash. I headed to my room to recover.

I wanted to ask my father about the magazine. I felt that there was something horribly wrong that such things existed and wondered what was wrong with my father that he owned it. In the end, I couldn't ask him—it was too shameful—and I decided that for the rest of my life, I would never speak to anybody about it.

"I found a porn magazine in my garage," I told my friend Dale the next week. He was three years older than me and already in the grips of puberty. I knew this would impress him and I had gone back into the dungeon of sin to bring it to him. He went away with it to the bathroom for a long time. He didn't seem to be ashamed at all, but that didn't make me feel any better. I felt worse each time I looked at the pictures. And each time, I vowed that I would never look at them again, a pattern that continued into adulthood.

I am not a gluttonous, lustful, nasty, perverted, sexually liberated person. But it appears my shadow is. At least this was the conclusion my inner therapist was coming to.

In adolescence, I'd formed a determinedly virtuous idea of sex: that it was supposed to be the method by which two souls connect, the gateway to a beautiful paradise. In fifth grade, I'd been told by an animated film that "when a man and a woman love each other very, very much, they want to be as close as they possibly can." And I took this to heart. When I first started having sex, I used to say things like, "Wow, I really felt us going to another place together" or "For a minute there, I felt like we were one being." I wasn't even trying to be funny—I meant these things. Or at least I was saying what I thought I was supposed to say. Finally, one of the girls I hooked up with in university told me, "Micah, it's okay to just say that was a really good fuck."

Then she told me she enjoyed rape fantasies. She wanted me to pin her arms down and she would protest in a believable fashion. I was not supposed to stop. I had never had rapist fantasies, but I found myself enjoying it. I really sunk into the role, though I could never quite fully abandon myself to it. If my performance had been captured on film, I think it would have been excoriated in the press. I would have been accused of "wooden acting." I was telling a friend about this recently and he shared with me an ex-girlfriend's demands, which were even more extreme.

"She wanted me to punch her," he said. "Like really hit her, with my fist." He showed me his fist. "And I couldn't do it. But then I thought to myself, I don't want to be able to do that, you know? One should be glad he can't ever fully abandon himself to that." I agreed, adding that enjoying punching one's girlfriend is not the textbook scenario of a healthy shadow integration. But, although I wasn't about to go out and purchase a full-body latex outfit, I started to think a kinky shadow side might not be such a bad thing.

Jung grew up as the son of a priest, so he inherited a strong fear of sin. When he was twelve years old, he was gazing up at a cathedral on a sunny summer day. "The roof of the cathedral glittered, the sun sparkling from the new, brightly glazed tiles," Jung wrote in his memoir. "I was overwhelmed by the beauty of the sight, and thought: 'The world is beautiful and the church is beautiful, and God made all this and sits above it far away in a blue sky on a golden throne and . . .'" But right there, before the narrative could continue in little Jung's mind, he stopped himself, forcibly shunting his brain so that it would not go forward with the thought that was to come next. He didn't yet know the full shape of the thought, but his instinct told him it was going to be very naughty, and sacrilegious.

This unrealized story was at the forefront of his mind for many days, like a video persistently on pause. As I read this account—it goes on for pages—I couldn't for the life of me predict what was going to happen next. But here's a hint: Think about the word "throne" and *all* its meanings.

Finally, after three days of willfully constipating his brain so that the next thought could not emerge, he finally let it drop: "God sits on His golden throne, high above the world—and from under the throne an enormous turd falls upon the sparkling new roof, shatters it, and breaks the walls of the cathedral asunder."

So that was it: God shat on the church. I'm not even religious, but I have to admit the image shocks me. It shocked Jung's descendents too, who tried to have the section removed altogether from Jung's posthumously published memoir. They settled finally on altering Jung's words so that it would read as politely as possible.

Jung's latter-day analysis of this fantasy was that his unconscious was telling him that God had a naughty side. As a result, he came to the opinion that if believers—including his father—never discussed or confronted that fact, how could they be Christians with any integrity?

As an adolescent, Jung never stumbled upon any of his father's pornographic magazines. But he did read *Faust*, which at the time made him feel dirty and awakened in a similar way.

In Goethe's closet drama, Dr. Faust picks up a poodle on the street and brings it home. Little does he know that the poodle is actually the Devil, named Mephistopheles. Faust signs a blood pact with the poodle Devil, and then goes on to seduce a young woman, accidentally aids her in poisoning and killing her mother, kills her brother in a duel, and knocks her up with a baby she eventually drowns. At the end, though, Faust is redeemed and allowed into heaven.

"*Faust* struck a chord in me and pierced me through in a way that I could not but regard as personal," Jung wrote. "Most of all, it awakened in me the problem of opposites, of good and evil, of mind and matter, of light and darkness. Faust, the inept, purblind philosopher, encounters the dark side of his being, his sinister shadow, Mephistopheles, who in spite of his negating disposition represents the true spirit of life as against the arid scholar who hovers on the brink of suicide."

So, according to Jung then, Faust could only really live once he had become one with evil for a while, sating his dark desires.

Lust and aggression are not amazingly unique shadow qualities for me to possess. I would venture to say they are two of the most common and that most people feel shame around them.

As far as sex goes, our personal fetishes are usually our most private secrets, and if they are unveiled to the public, they are usually met with the hatred of millions projecting their own shame. In secret, of course, those millions go watch the video online.

Our leaders are not allowed to be lustful beings. They should be married and have children, but anything other than that is suspect. Sex is not clean, no matter how much we try to make it or present it as such to our children. Another essay in *Meeting the Shadow* takes on this topic. "Sexuality is still demonised in our day," writes Adolf Guggenhul-Craig. "All attempts to render it completely harmless and to present it as something 'completely natural' flounder and fail. To modern man, sexuality in certain forms continues to appear as something evil and sinfully sinister."

In contrast to Western Christianity, Jung was surprised to find on a visit to India that the Buddhists had integrated sexuality into their religion. Upon visiting a pagoda in Konarak, a small town on the Bay of Bengal, he discovered that the temple was "covered from base to pinnacle with exquisitely obscene sculptures." A Hindu scholar told him the pornographic sculptures were "a means to achieve spiritualization." Jung pointed out that some young men nearby were simply gaping at the statues and that they were "scarcely undergoing spiritualization at the moment, but were much more likely having their heads

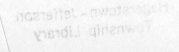

filled with sexual fantasies." The scholar replied that this was the point—the young men needed to be reminded of their sexual desires so that they could know them and eventually not be ruled by them. If they remained unconscious of them, they may never be able to do so.

I had seen the sculpted bodies of my father's pornography, but that didn't seem to have worked for me. In fact, it had the opposite effect, perhaps because what I was learning—in the darkness of the cold garage—was that sexuality was something to hide. As an adult, my inner therapist concluded, I was still repressed and wanted to be seen as an upright and moral person, which I thought excluded lust, as well as what I called "being a mean person" (i.e., normal, healthy assertiveness).

The irony is that when a person creates a scrubbed-clean persona, he usually starts to seem sinister. Mr. Rogers, for example, in his cardigan, talking really nice to kids on television, was one of the most prolific educators of his time and just a downright swell guy. He taught goodness and he seemed to reflect that kind of behavior on his show. But somewhere in my memory, there is the idea floating around that Mr. Rogers was uncovered as a pedophile. Some research proves this to be untrue, but why was it so easy to believe that rumor? Meanwhile, the most common response from neighbors of serial killers or people who end up shooting their spouse, children, and then themselves is, "He just seemed like a normal, average guy. Never made any trouble."

A friend of mine who has edited several documentaries told me that if you show your subject as being only a kindhearted hero, the audience tended to hate him. "They want to see his flaws," he said, "because that's what they can relate to."

"Every form of addiction is bad," Jung wrote, "no matter whether the narcotic be alcohol or morphine or idealism. We must beware of thinking of good and evil as absolute opposites." Later, he adds: "Nothing can spare us the torment of ethical decision. Nevertheless, harsh as it may sound, we must have the freedom in some circumstances to avoid the known moral good and do what is considered to be evil, if our ethical decision so requires."

So how does a person such as myself access his uglier side? Not easily. As Jung says, "To become conscious of [the shadow] involves recognizing the dark aspects of the personality as present and real. This act is the essential condition for any kind of self-knowledge, and it therefore, as a rule, meets with considerable resistance."

So then why bother? I mean, who needs to be looking in the mirror every day trying to convince himself that he's an asshole and a pervert? Well, the problem, as my father once explained to me, is that the shadow has a nasty way of coming out anyway—even if you're trying to hold it back—and it's usually worse if you don't learn to embrace it consciously. You, like Dr. Faust, might "accidentally" get a girl pregnant, poison her mother, and drive her to kill her baby. Happens *all* the time. It's better, Jung thought, to accept your shadow qualities and figure out ways of bringing them into your life in nondestructive ways.

The other major pitfall of not owning your shadow is that you tend to inexplicably attract people who act it out for you. If you're a doormat and your shadow side is more aggressive, you'll find yourself constantly surrounded by pushy, self-centered assholes. If you're always making cynical jokes and are disallowing the more direct, honest part of your personality, you'll have super-earnest co-workers visiting your cubicle at work and never leaving you alone. And, no matter how many hundreds of miles you move away from these people, there they are again with different names and faces.

Additionally, my father told me, you may start to see your shadow qualities in another person and because you fear those qualities in yourself, they become an overemphasized aspect of the way you see that person. Thus, whenever in that person's presence, you enter into something of a delusional cloud. Jung called this projection.

"The effect of projection is to isolate the subject from his environment, since instead of a real relation to it there is now only an illusory one," he wrote. "Projections change the world into the replica of one's own unknown face."

I consider my friend William to be exceptionally sexually liberated. Although he has always carried his hulking Greek emperor-like physique with a fair dose of introverted humility, he does flirt everywhere he goes, with both men and women. He's had encounters with people younger than himself, his own age, and older. It's almost as if the man has no boundaries whatsoever when it comes to sex. He doesn't believe in monogamy and, on occasion, he has omitted certain information from his lovers to maintain this lifestyle. For a long time, I looked at his behavior and thought it was immoral. Still, he was a loyal friend to me and as much as I sometimes detested his behavior, I also loved him. The contradiction I felt was unbearable. There must be something wrong with him, I kept thinking. How can it be right to be so *lascivious*? I finally confronted him, laying bare my opinion of him in a letter, to which he responded with a very brief reply—"Goddamn, Micah!"—and then we didn't speak for almost a year.

My shadow confrontation with my inner therapist happened to coincide with this lapse in our friendship, so I was conveniently able to ask myself: WWJD? (No, not What Would Jesus Do, but What Would Jung Do?) If Jung were in the same position, I thought, he would ask himself what he is disallowing in his own personality that leads him to hold such a strong judgment of another person.

Hello, my name is Micah Toub, and I am a boundless slut with no scruples. Pushy, too.

———

The confrontation with my shadow came to a head one day while I was looking at pornography online while Beth was out.

As I was partaking in this sinful pastime, my father suddenly popped into my mind. This was not as troubling as the vision of my mother while I was masturbating as a teen, but it was still somewhat, well, distracting.

I started thinking about how he had told me once that to accept one's shadow, one needs to find healthy ways of integrating it into one's life. And I remembered reading a dire warning of Jung's: "Everyone carries a shadow," he said, "and the less it is embodied in the individual's conscious life, the blacker and denser it is. At all counts, it forms an unconscious snag, thwarting our most well-meant intentions."

Based on a scientific survey I'd taken of my friends—both male and female—my consumption of pornography was average, but I still felt an immense amount of shame about it. As I fed my compulsion, my heart would race and my senses would all go hazy just like when I was a kid shoving Ding Dongs into my face. I'd always have this sense that I was doing something wrong, I would be caught, and my life as I knew it would be over. Afterward, I'd sit there depressed and half-undressed. I was Half Naked Man, but I definitely didn't feel like a superhero. There'd be a picture of a woman in her backyard doing things with garden appliances still on the screen and I'd start to wonder who she was. Is that how she makes a living? What the hell is going on? Then I'd pull my clothes back on and rush to the cupboard to eat an entire box of cookies.

It was irrational, but it was how I felt. And, my inner therapist hastened to add, it was not a healthy integration. So this time I finally decided enough was enough, and owned up to this aspect of my shadow. It took me awhile to figure out where to start, but I was at my computer, so I decided the best way to be my shadow was to write pornographic stories. I got seriously into the pursuit and became a prolific Harlequin hopeful for a while. At night in bed, I'd read Beth the stories and find ways to turn them into something like reality, or, as Jung might say, embody my libido into my conscious life. And in a short time, I came to see that my so-called lascivious friend William was simply doing that same thing.

Dealing with aggression was a more difficult matter. Was I supposed to just walk around looking for people to pick fights with?

But I remembered something my mother had said while discussing my Morpheus dream. "You don't actually have to kill people," she said. "It's more about getting to the essence of the killer."

Going out and murdering people, my mother explained, is overcompensating. If the killer were able to figure out what he wants and what he's trying to accomplish in a metaphorical way by the killing and instead live his life in a "killing" manner, then he would not have to actually kill.

I thought back on her question: what would it mean to face a situation with a shotgun? The point would not be to go out to the gun shop and actually purchase a weapon, but instead to assume the power of that object. I decided to still go out shopping, but for something a bit less sinister—jeans.

To test out my shadow, I walked into the trendiest men's clothing store I could find, armed with my invisible shotgun. The store was exactly the type of place where I hated to shop, because whenever I did I'd be pushed around by a salesperson too cool to help me and I'd end up buying something I didn't really want.

As the door slammed shut behind me, I strode in like Clint Eastwood and stood in the center of the store, giving enough

time for everyone to turn around and see me. That's right, moth-
erfuckers, I thought to myself, I'm here to *shop*.

"I need some jeans," I announced to three staff chatting at the
cash register. They quickly negotiated among themselves who was
going to help out this badass that had just entered the store. The
guy who got picked took me over to a stack of jeans and suggested
I try a pair on.

"I don't like those," I said, nearly snarling at him.

"Okay, no problem," he chirped and took me around until we
found some I did want to try on.

As I was trying to squeeze myself into a pair that was too small
for me, he called over the door to ask if I was okay.

"I need a larger size," I demanded, without apology. As I waited
for him to fetch another pair, it occurred to me that he was a very
friendly person.

"You're really helpful," I told the guy when I finally came out to
look in the mirror.

"Well, that's my job. I'm here to help," he said.

"I know. It's just . . . normally I find salespeople really pushy
and arrogant."

"Really? Not here, right?"

"Oh, it's probably been my fault. Now I'm trying to be more
pushy myself to see if that makes a difference. I'm integrating my
shadow."

He stared at me silently for a moment.

"I'm the son of two Jungian psychologists," I said.

"Oh!" He laughed. "That's hilarious. My dad is a psychologist
too."

Needless to say, I walked out of there with exactly the pair of jeans I wanted. So it wasn't the greatest conflict that I'll have to face in the oncoming years, but it was a start.

After shopping, in celebration, I went home and looked at loads of porn. I'd had enough self-discovery for one day. And anyway, it was shadow research. Not to mention completely useless.

My father would be proud.

7

The Ally

(A Spirit Guide in the Suburbs)

"Would you be freaked out if I started meditating to contact my spirit guide?" I asked Beth one day in bed.

I'd been spending a lot of time in that bed after getting run down by a car on my bike, a collision that shattered one of my ankles and broke my shin bone. A lot of strange things had been passing through my head—the same one that torpedoed into the windshield—after a few days confined by a cast and high on Percocet.

"Yes," she said automatically.

"Really?"

"Yes, I would."

That day, I'd been thinking specifically about something my mother told me years ago when I was a boy—that I possessed an Ally, a spirit guide. At the time, it was something I accepted with

childish naivete and growing up, it had become the closest thing
to a religious belief that was passed down to me from my parents.
Over the years, I'd come to be skeptical and what you might call
a nonobservant spirit guide owner, but after surviving near-death,
I started to wonder whether maybe something *was* looking after
me. Maybe there was a spirit of some sort protecting me. And
now I was feeling defensive.

"But why?" I asked Beth. "I mean, it's just meditation."

"Micah, the fact that you're asking me that question means
that you think I would get freaked out. And *that* freaks me out.
Yes, I'd be afraid that you'd get flakier and flakier and that I'd get
more and more conservative. That's what you expected me to say,
isn't it?"

I envisioned a future where Beth, a permanent scowl on her
face and wearing a nun's habit, encounters me sitting on a cushion in the living room, blonde dreadlocks obscuring my face as I
commune with my spirit posse.

Beth reminded me that I'd once told her I feared we would
become like my father and his second wife. Although this former
stepmother of mine married a Jungian psychologist, she never
really bought into the more spiritual side of my father's personal
practices. When they finally broke up, my father told me that during one of their last fights she'd said to him, "I just can't grow old
with a man who owns a Tarot deck." I regretted the comparison
now.

"Well, I'm going to do the meditation," I said. "But don't
worry."

Beth rolled over and we fell asleep.

For most people, the word "ally" will bring to mind war, or more specifically will evoke the Allies—U.S., Britain, Canada, etc.— during the Second World War. But this is not the case for me, my family, or any of the former hippies who read Carlos Castaneda in the 1970s and, despite the inhalation of enormous amounts of marijuana, still remember it. For all of us in this group, *Ally* is foremost the name of the spirit who is contacted by a shaman for guidance and assistance in healing the wounded souls of his village. This kind of ally has been around for centuries. Of course, the day I first became aware of the concept, in the early 1980s, I wouldn't know to call it "Ally." I was only eight years old.

It was a Saturday in the summer, a sunny day that I'd mostly spent shooting water out of the hose, gunning down grasshoppers that sat peacefully atop the woodpile in our backyard. Some of them I captured between my cupped hands, taking them over to the lawn as they knocked around against my palms. I held them down and staked them into the grass with a one-inch nail. This sadistic compulsion to annihilate and torture all of grasshopper-kind was perhaps a compensation for my usual hyperpacifism toward humans. Or, it could have been the result of watching Luke Skywalker de-limb bad guys one too many times. In any case, I enjoyed it so much that after that summer the grasshoppers never came back.

When evening rolled around, my parents decided we'd go out

for dinner, which pretty much made it a perfect day as far as I was concerned. We packed ourselves into the silver Subaru station wagon and fastened our seatbelts. My father was driving, my mother in the passenger seat, and Andreya and I in the back. I leaned my forehead against the window to watch the neighborhood drift by. The only difference between all the houses on our block was the two colors that covered them: blue with dark blue trim, gray with mauve trim, black with white trim. What was life like inside those other-colored houses, I wondered. Was there anything about the colors that could give any hint? Ours was yellow with brown trim, like peanut butter and banana sandwiches, which I ate a lot of. As we passed, the kids who lived in those other houses stopped whatever game they were playing to turn and watch as the Toub family headed off for the evening. I was happy because that night I didn't have to be one of those kids stuck in their houses. And I was already thinking about tartar sauce.

We used to go out to dinner about once a month. The other twenty-nine days, my parents cooked cornmeal-y casseroles or veggie burgers, brown rice and peas as sides. But when we went out, my sister and I could order whatever we wanted. We usually went to a seafood chain restaurant called Skipper's, whose walls and ceilings were covered with faux retro life preservers, plastic pirate booty, fish nets, paintings of mermaids—the kind of mishmash kitsch décor perfected in the suburbs of Denver in the early 1980s. I don't know any longer what I would order—only that it was deep-fried, with a side of "Captain Coleslaw." My sister always ordered the lobster. Her tastes had a way of uncannily aligning with what was most expensive on the menu, a habit that didn't fit so well with our modest means. Nonetheless, on these monthly occasions, my parents indulged her.

On this particular outing, however, a strange thing occurred. Strange, unless you know my family.

Ten minutes after we'd departed, about halfway there, we were passing by Donkey Hill, grooved and ravaged by last winter's sledding season. I remembered the rush of going down it, the most thrilling thing on Earth—besides tartar sauce, I thought, and wondered: Can you eat it all by itself?

But then.

I heard my mother mumble something and my father immediately pulled the car over to the shoulder. We were not at Skipper's yet and not even at an intersection.

"What is it?" my father asked.

"I'm not sure yet," my mother answered, very seriously. "Something's wrong."

I started to worry, concerned about her health. I wondered if maybe she had a headache or a stomachache. Then I thought maybe she had cancer.

"What are you feeling?" my father asked.

"Let me just listen for a minute," she said, then closed her eyes and put her chin down to her chest. My father watched her, and for a few moments the only sound was my mother's uneven breathing.

Then she spoke, slowly, emphasizing each word as if she were reading from a faraway billboard. "Something bad is going to happen," she said.

My mother is going to die, I thought. I started envisioning the future without her, how my life would change completely. My father would let us eat white bread with Jiffy, but it wouldn't be fun that way, with Mom dead.

"I don't think we should go to the restaurant," she said.

My father silently nodded. "Okay," he said, making a U-turn.

"No!" my sister called out from the back. "Mom, *please* can we still go? Nothing bad is going happen. *Please.*"

"I'm sorry, Andreya, but I just think that we should go back home. I don't know yet exactly why, but I feel very strongly about it."

A *psyche*-ache.

"Kids," my father said, glancing at us in the rearview mirror, "sometimes you have a feeling or hear a voice inside of you that tells you that you should or should not do something, and your mother and I are making an effort to follow that more closely. In fact, if you ever have a feeling like that you should tell us."

"I feel like we should go to the restaurant," Andreya said. My father ignored her.

Meanwhile, I was completely amazed by what had just happened. My mother had been contacted by some all-knowing presence—could it be that The Force really did exist?—and it was affecting our real life. It was like a choose-your-own-adventure story, and in one version of our life, we had gone to the restaurant and had dinner and who knows what, the route we always chose. But now we were actually choosing that other one, the one that included magical beings and visits from E.T.

I pressed my head against the window again and looked out at all those houses. Their near-identical faces seemed even more mysterious than before. Something was different. Something very integral had changed. My mother had psychic powers.

A year later, my mother told me about her Ally, and mine.

"Micah," she said to me on that fateful day, "before you were born, when you were still inside my womb, I had a dream about you. In it, you were a small boy, but very wise. And then, when you were born, when I saw you for the first time, I *knew* right away that you had the sun inside of you." She patted the center of my chest, just below my ribcage and above my little boy paunch. "That sun is your Ally, and it is there to love and protect you. I have one too."

She told me this the morning after I'd had what most parents would call a nightmare, but which mine diagnosed as an "ally dream" and a sign that I was coming into touch with my big "s" Self.

When I woke from the dream in the middle of the night, I ran to my father's side of the bed. He was the one I'd appointed for bad dream duty.

My father's a deep sleeper, so he was always disoriented when I woke him. For a few seconds, he had this panicked look on his face like he didn't know who I was or even who he was. It was not very reassuring fresh from nightmare-land. But then it came back to him: *I am a psychologist. I live in the suburbs with my family. I have a son. This must be him here right now.* He said my name in his soft voice, wrapped his naked body in a giant yellow polyester robe, and brought me back to bed, where he sat down next to me and listened to my dream. As I told him the nightmare, I held tightly to Tom Tom, the stuffed koala bear who hadn't left my side since I was five. Mimicking my father, who also had a stuffed koala at his bedside, I had chosen it as my animal guardian.

In the dream I'd been chased throughout the house by an invisible presence. At first, I was in the kitchen and it was hiding under the table. I sensed that the thing was powerful enough to kill me, so I took off up the stairs. I felt it chasing me, but whenever I would turn around, I would see nothing there. I ran down the hallway and into my parents' bedroom and shook them but they wouldn't wake up. I gave up and headed back downstairs to the living room, and, for a few moments, I didn't know where the evil thing had gone. Then I looked out the window. There it was, a basketball-sized sphere floating just outside, over the front lawn. The sphere was stunningly bright but shadowy at the same time, the same effect as when you stare at the sun and the intense whiteness moves across your cornea, creating ripples of black as it swirls around. The sphere didn't have eyes, but I could tell that it was looking at me, waiting for me to do something. I was less frightened with the window separating us, so I stared at it for a few seconds before turning away to make sure the rest of the room was safe. When I looked back it was gone.

My memory of the dream is vivid not only because it became an important one for me—what Jung would call a "big dream"— but also because the next day at breakfast my father asked me if I would draw it for him. He brought me some crayons and thin, typewriter paper, and I illustrated the dream in four panels, with narration in pencil. He still has "My Dream" in his Micah file to this day, next to annual personality assessments, IQ tests, and other highly telling drawings and writings. He got very excited when he examined the last panel of the dream, the sphere as seen through the living room window, and ran off to get something. When he returned, he was carrying one of his Jung books, which he opened to a picture of a circle split into four quadrants. He pointed out that in my drawing, the sphere from my dream was also split into four sections by the windowpane. "This," he said, "is a representation of your Self." He was smiling. "See," he said, pointing back and forth between my drawing and the one in the book.

What my father was showing me in Jung's book was a mandala, the circular art form of Hindu origin that has been around for over two thousand years. Jung got hooked on them in his early forties, back in 1919. He was in a dark period of his life, after he'd split with Freud and before he'd established a new philosophical framework that he could believe in. At the time, he was lecturing at a university, but couldn't get himself excited any longer about the ideas he'd been teaching. Although he knew he was putting his career in jeopardy, and that he might never become a full professor, in 1918 he quit his job to have, as he explains in his memoirs, a "confrontation with the unconscious." He meant his own unconscious; he was going to explore the caves of his own head, because, as he puts it, "I could not expect of my patients something I did not dare to do myself." He'd already come up with the idea of archetypes, inspired by the dream he lied about to Freud, and now he was hoping to find some subjective evidence of these common psychic forms.

From the outside, this noble quest would have looked slightly

ridiculous. Some of Jung's practices at that time included talking
to himself; listening for voices and then writing down what they
said; closing his eyes and going on visual journeys that at least one
time included a "dwarf with a leathery skin"; building a miniature
village out of stones; and then, finally, drawing the mandalas. He
drew one in his diary every morning upon waking. Jung admitted
he felt foolish about doing all this, but it finally did lead him to a
breakthrough.

One day, after receiving a particularly troubling letter—he
doesn't say from whom, but his description intimates it was from
Sabina Spielrein—he drew his daily mandala, and, comparing it
with the one from the day before, discovered that the state of
his psyche, shaken by the letter, was illustrated in the change in
the mandala. The second one's outer surface had been ruptured.
After observing this same effect in other instances, Jung concluded that mandalas were "cryptograms concerning the state of
the self which were presented to me anew each day."

Jung then went spiraling into a mandala craze, became a man-
dalahead, if you will. He started seeing circles everywhere: ancient
religions worshipped the sun; the ground plans of Rome, Jeru-
salem, and Washington, DC, were all circular; the solar system
rotated in a circular fashion around the sun; Christ wore a halo
over his head; and the most mysterious objects in the world—
UFOs—were almost always depicted as flying disks. The legend
of Brahma, an Indian creation myth, says that the god stood on
a thousand-petaled lotus and turned his eyes to the four points
of the compass, taking his bearings before he began with the
creation. By doing this, he created a circle with four quadrants,
divided by a cross. This was a common image among creation

myths and for Jung became symbolic of the human need for psychic orientation and thus the pictograph of the Self.

This is what was running through my father's head as he looked at my drawing of a sphere cut into four by the windowpanes. He was so worked up about it because I had unwittingly drawn a rudimentary sketch of the Self. Here was proof from his own son that these symbols really did lurk inside every person. The existence of the collective unconscious was once again vindicated.

I, on the other hand, wasn't sure how to take the news exactly. I was excited by the fact that I had by accident done something that my father found worthy of so much fuss, but I didn't know what it meant about me. All I could figure was that I'd had a very important dream and things seemed to be going as planned. *I had psychic powers too.* That's when my mother, who'd been in the kitchen during the discussion, mentioned nonchalantly—as if she were telling me that I used to eat the peels off of oranges—the whole bit about the sun in my chest.

A week or so after I'd had the ally dream and drawn the pictures for my father, my mother told me more about my Ally as she put me to bed.

"Your sun will always love you," she said.

"Even when I do something bad?"

"Yes, even then. Always. At any moment in your life, no matter what else is happening, there is always something that loves you. That's your Ally."

"But what if I do something *really* bad, like kill somebody?"

"Even if you kill somebody, your Ally will love you, entirely and completely."

No matter what I did, even if I became an evil Russian spy, there was a being that loved me. It was a reassuring thought.

"And," she said, "if you're ever in a bad situation or need some advice, your Ally can give you guidance."

"How does it do that?"

"You just ask it. Close your eyes and ask the question that you want answered. Then just listen. It may come as a voice or it may come as an image."

"So can it give me answers to math problems?"

"No, it's more about feeling things, not thinking things. It can help you make big decisions." After a pause she added, "And by the way, don't go killing anyone!"

———

After many hours of surgery following my bike accident, I spent the night in the hospital. I didn't sleep though, kept awake by the combination of an IV drip that made me constantly have to pee and a drug that I was on that made peeing nearly impossible. I had a lot of time to consider the fact that I had almost died. (In fact, had I not been wearing a helmet, you would not be reading this book.) In my head, I kept going over the events of the morning.

Very early, before heading to work on my bike, I had picked

up a rental car that Beth and I were going to use to drive up to Beth's family cottage that evening. I was stressed about getting some writing done that weekend, and as I drove the car away from the parking lot, I had a thought of just staying home and spending two days on a writing marathon like Jack Kerouac had done at the Chelsea Hotel to finish off *On the Road*. The idea was very appealing, but I decided it was too late to change plans.

I was driving home recklessly out of frustration, slamming my foot on the accelerator every time the light turned green. And as I was speeding underneath a bridge on the final leg of the trip home, I remembered that time, over twenty years before, when my family was heading to Skipper's and my mother had made us turn back. I wondered if the way I was feeling about staying home was the same as what she'd been feeling back then. I had a more concrete and rational reason for wanting to change my mind and I wasn't hearing any disembodied voice, but, ultimately, *something* was telling me to turn back, a something that I was ignoring. What happens when you don't follow that feeling? I thought as I drove, visions of Beth and me bloody on the highway coming into my head. But I decided, in the end, to brush all that aside. I left the rental car in my driveway and set out for work on my bike.

As I squeezed drops of urine into the jug that night in the hospital, I started to consider whether this Ally of mine had even tried to warn me. Maybe I had ignored it for so long that it was now screaming at me, forcing me back onto some path of the Self that I had neglected for too long. It suddenly seemed very important to me that I have a more profound explanation of why I was still alive other than that I cascaded against the hood of the car at a fortuitous angle.

Also, that drug I was on was morphine.

———

Trying to pin down in what way the Ally exists is tricky, which becomes clear if you read Carlos Castaneda's *The Teachings of Don Juan,* the book that got my parents interested in this business in the first place. I'd snagged it from my mother's library when I was a teenager, but hadn't read it until just a couple years before the accident.

When Castaneda takes his first round of peyote while apprenticing with his Mexican guru don Juan, he gets so high that every time he drinks water he sees himself growing a mane of vibrantly colored fibers. Castaneda starts playing with a dog who also drinks water and who also acquires a glowing mane just like his. They commune in a secret language of twitches and jumps. The next day, Castaneda is chagrined to learn from the other men who were around at the time that he had—in reality—just been puking, running after the dog of one of the men and even pissing on it. Not sparing Castaneda his dignity, the owner of the dog also finally reveals: "My dog got even though; he pissed on you too!"

But don Juan assures Castaneda that it doesn't matter what the men saw. "You played with 'him,'" he says, referring to the spirit of the peyote. Even if in "ordinary reality" Castaneda was just being urinated on by a dog, the events of "nonordinary reality" that Castaneda had experienced were just as true.

Later, don Juan teaches Castaneda to grow the peyote—which he calls the "Devil's Weed"—and gives him a portion of it from the root that induces a hallucination where Castaneda experiences flying high over the desert. He eventually lands, and when he wakes, finds himself miles away from where he started—naked, since don Juan had made him take off all his clothes beforehand. Castaneda, a rational man of science from Los Angeles, insists that it is not possible that he was actually flying, that it was all just the effects of the peyote, and that if a friend had watched him during his drug trip, he would not have seen Castaneda actually flying like a bird but just shaking on the ground. "It is useless to talk that way," responds don Juan. "If your friend, or anybody else, takes the second portion of the weed all he can do is fly. Now, if he had simply watched you, he might have seen you flying, or he might not. That depends on the man."

Even as a child, I understood that if you cut open my ribcage, you would not find a miniature sun in there. But in the middle of the night in the hospital, I started to wonder whether on some plane my Ally did exist.

When I woke in the morning after a couple hours of sleep in my hospital room, I used my new crutches to hobble my way over to the payphone outside my room. I called my mother and told her about the feeling I'd had the day of the accident, the one I'd not listened to. She agreed it had been a forewarning and possibly from my Ally.

"But Mom?" I said.

"Yes, Micah?"

"How can I be absolutely sure that it was my Ally? I mean, I'm not sure I believe in it to begin with." Saying this felt like a betrayal.

"You don't have to believe in it," she said, unfazed. "It just is."

"I know you always say that, but if I am to believe in it, I want some proof." I expected her to continue to find some way to convince me that of course I have an Ally. But she took another tack—not exactly reverse psychology, but, I don't know, maybe *inverse* psychology.

"Why don't you ask *it*?" she suggested.

"You mean, ask my Ally if it exists?"

Yes. Do an Ally meditation and have a dialogue with it. Find out in what way it does or doesn't exist for you."

"Wouldn't talking to my Ally be defeating the purpose of questioning its existence?"

"Maybe it won't answer you," she said, chuckling, presumably at how silly I was being.

Many years before, during that first awkward trip home with Beth, her more rational presence had made it startlingly apparent to me how high in metaland my family often floated. At the first dinner, Peter talked about how much he liked to drink lattes—normal enough—but my mother and he quickly turned this to a phenomenological discussion of addictions and what one's inner self is really trying to accomplish by substance use. Peter's son, a college student at the time, spoke of the metaphysical quality of pushing one's body to the limit (aka, doing beer bongs until you're passing out on the toilet). This was not exactly the small talk expected upon meeting a new boyfriend's family for the first time.

As much as it embarrassed me, I also liked it. I reveled in all the metatalk and seeking meaning beneath the mundane. Our conversations were often trying to figure out what it all meant, what we believed in, and what our purpose was in this life. When Beth and I retired to my room, I wondered for the first time what she believed.

Once we were settled in bed, I pulled the sheet up over our heads to create an otherworldly atmosphere. Then, I popped the big question: "Do you believe in God?"

"What?"

"I mean, do you believe in anything supernatural? You know, like what's your spirituality?" It wasn't even that I felt I had figured out my own beliefs, but I thought about these things and I wanted to know if she did too.

"I don't know. I guess I'm agnostic, since I don't really believe in God, but I don't know that God doesn't exist."

"Oh," I said. Her answer seemed so conventional to me at the time. I thought then that this might be a deal breaker.

"Well, there is something," she said. "The green mist."

"The green mist?"

"Well, I've always imagined that there's this green mist that everything is made of and that when you die, you are still part of it."

"That sounds kind of Buddhist. Why is it green?"

"Green's my favorite color."

That silenced me. I was simultaneously pleased that I had drawn this out of her and also suddenly caught on the other side of the fence, wondering how she could profess to believe something so absurd. Why green? I laugh at the reaction now—as if there's a nonabsurd image of the supernatural.

Later, I pieced together where this idea of Beth's came from. Besides being Beth's favorite color, green is also the color of her family's cottage, and of course the trees up there in the north of Ontario. At dawn in the early summer, a fog fills the chilled air, settling on the lake before the rising sun evaporates it. Beth once told me that for a long time she was afraid to swim in the middle of the lake because she believed there was an enormous monster down there that would rise to devour her. These images formed a kind of spirituality for Beth, a mythology, one centered in family and nature.

Over the years, though, I came to understand that Beth, at least consciously, is foremost a firm believer in deliberate choice, in decision making that comes from a clear head and not from anyone or anything else, especially not some magical voice from beyond. Not that I was in the habit of taking guidance from disembodied voices, but I wondered what would happen if, while meditating, my Ally did speak to me, providing me with some revolutionary key to finding that elusive road to enlightenment, to nirvana. What if it told me that I must put my hair into a ponytail, wear baggy pants, and follow the *energy*, man?

My own doubts about the Ally began at the same time that I started writing poetry about how society—and my father—were "keeping me down." At that age, fifteen or so, I was comfortable sharing almost anything with my mother, but not this uncertainty. How do you tell your mother that you're not sure if you believe in her religion? Occasionally, "my sun" would come up in conversation and I'd try to play along.

One day over brunch we were going over a problem I was having at school, and she told me that I should trust my instincts. "If you really pay attention, you'll see that you *know* the answer already."

"You mean, from my sun?" I said, my voice getting quiet.

"*Yes*," my mother beamed.

I'd brought it up so that this connection between us wouldn't evaporate completely, but the truth was it hadn't felt like there was a sun around for years. Every once in a while, I'd be in a really tight spot and close my eyes, asking my Ally what I should do. Sometimes a random image would pop into my head, but it would be so far from a literal response that I'd often just shrug it off. I was too lazy to interpret all the random symbols. If there was an Ally there on the other side of that line, it was understandably pissed off at this point with all the prank calls.

Then, one day, out of nowhere my mother said to me, "My analyst told me a long time ago that when you became a teenager, you would forget about your Ally." I was simultaneously flattered that she and her analyst had been talking about the state of my spirit guide behind my back, and also relieved that she had come to her own way of understanding the shift, that I could put off breaking my loss of faith to her. But then she added, "He said that eventually you would be curious again and it would come back to you."

My mother's analyst was not completely wrong. I did forget about my Ally for a few years, and then I did get curious again later in high school, via the daily smoking of marijuana. At some point mid-joint, I told my friends about the sun, about what my mother had told me when I was little. Being from relatively normal families, and at the moment, very high, they were impressed by my Ally story. They started calling me "Sunboy" or "Sunny," and drew suns next to my name on notes and letters. My favorite shirt, which I wore one time when we tripped on acid, was an orange and yellow tie-dye with a giant picture of a sun that took up the whole front. None of this was done ironically. On the contrary, my cosmic identification fit exactly into our philosophical speculations at the time. We were curious about souls, about what exists beneath the skin, about the transcendental connections between everything. And as we discussed these subjects, we passed around a bong that was three feet high and blue, which we called Moby.

However, as much I ever talked *about* my Ally, I wasn't ever talking *to* my Ally, or meditating with it properly. I was fetishizing it, wearing it as an accessory like my sun shirt, as an affectation that says I am spiritual in my own way without needing organized religion as a crutch. My use of drugs helped me to access Castaneda's nonordinary reality. I was exploring sideways versions of reality, discovering lucid truths about the universe and laughing at the weirdness of elbows, but I wasn't truly communicating with any imaginary friend.

In the moments when I took it the most seriously, I believed that my Ally was protecting me, giving me good luck, maybe unconsciously guiding me. I wasn't willing to do the work necessary to maintain a connection with it, but I accepted the benefits that it might be bestowing on me. Like a Christian who no longer believes that Jesus saves, but who, in a desperate situation, will put in a half-ironic prayer to the Son who might be listening, I believed in my sun just enough to keep the idea around *just in case*.

I am Jewish, a fact that is evident to some people based on my first name. Micah was a Hebrew prophet from the eighth century B.C., and has his own book in the Old Testament. But I wasn't named after a Jewish prophet because of my parents' Judaism. The reason for my name goes back to the dream my mother had about me before I was born. "In the dream, you were very wise," she told me. (I always imagined she saw me as a little boy sitting on a meditation cushion.) They wanted to pick a name for me that matched this prophecy of my mother's and they chose Micah because, as my mother later told me, "he seemed the most positive of the prophets."

Micah, I learned when I read the Book of Micah, foresaw that the city of Samaria would be annihilated because its people had stopped following God's law, though he said the obedient few would be spared and then thrive after everyone else was wiped out. Among prophets, I guess that passes for optimism.

My mother was actually born a Protestant, but she converted to Judaism after she married my father, an act motivated more from her own intellectual curiosity about religion than from the wish to align with my father's faith. My father's abnormal observance of Judaism gave a new meaning to "reformed," something he blames on his father.

Sixty years ago, Grandpa Toub had studied and practiced to perform his Bar Mitzvah. However, the big day left him feeling unsatisfied and after it was over, at some point between becoming a man and becoming a father, he decided he would never make his own son go through the same arduous process. Thus, the thousands of years of Judaism that led down into my family line were abruptly squashed.

Out of that void came my father: Bob Dylan listener, LSD experimenter, and Jungian philosopher. He married my mother: women's rights activist, macrobiotic fanatic, and self-proclaimed shamaness. The religion created out of their union was the do-it-yourself variety Americans have become experts at.

My father owned a simple wooden menorah, which was displayed in the living room. Sometimes, at Hanukah, we'd put candles in it and light them like normal Jews. Sometimes, we'd forget. Or, we'd light them for a few days, forget for a few days, then light them all on the last day. On Passover, we'd often have a special dinner, but instead of eating unleavened matzoh to remember the haste with which the Jews fled Egypt, we'd pass around a cornucopia of breads—rye, pumpernickel, olive, whole wheat—the largest variety of breads to grace our table all year long.

Christmas, meanwhile, was celebrated every year. We'd put up a tree, decorate it with homemade ornaments, and then my father would set up a ladder and put a star on the top, which he'd made out of cardboard and tinfoil. It was the Star of David. He was Jewish, after all.

Alongside these alt Judeo-Christian rituals were others that would come and go, brought in from faraway cultures, seemingly at random.

One morning, while I was sitting at the table eating a bowl of cereal when I was thirteen, my father came over from the living room and held a small red velvet pouch in front of me.

"Reach inside and think about the upcoming day," he demanded, eyes lit up with mischievous glee. (There were times when, as a teenager, I felt older than him.) I put down my spoon and did what he said. Inside the bag, I could feel cold, hard objects, rectangles a couple inches long, a little bit bigger than dominoes. They seemed to be each engraved on one side.

"Pull one out. But make sure to keep concentrating on the upcoming day."

Thinking about school, about eating lunch in the cafeteria, and about the fact that one of my so-called friends seemed to be avoiding me, I pulled one of the pieces out of the bag.

It was white, with one rough side and one smooth side. The smooth side had an engraving of a complicated mess of thick criss-crossing broken lines.

My father flipped through a small book.

"Oh. Hmm." He looked concerned.

"What is it?" I asked.

"This rune is called Suffering," he said, grinning sheepishly.

"Great."

"Don't worry. Suffering is not a bad thing. It's what comes before rebirth."

After that, my father pulled out his own rune and looked it up in the book. "Oh look, I got Strength," he said, and bounced over to the couch to record it in his rune diary.

The runes didn't hold my father's interest long, but if it wasn't that, we were throwing the I Ching—essentially the Chinese version of rune casting—or my mother and I were reading Tarot cards together.

My parents were, I can admit it, a little bit New Age. And, my mother *really* likes to wear purple. But I was never able to just put them in that box and dismiss them. They didn't burn incense, meditate, and then go about their lives pretending that these rituals somehow made them superior to the average working American. And my parents' ultimate goal was not to achieve some flaky version of inner peace or to be lost in a blissful haze while ignoring the darker sides of humanity. Like Jung, they were confronting the unconscious parts of their personalities—including the not-so-peace-loving ones—to be more fully aware and conscious.

Jung is sometimes called the forefather of the New Age, and while his philosophies have inspired people to broaden their ideas of spirituality, his concepts are used by some people in the same superficial and fetishistic way in which I wore the sun shirt while tripping on acid.

My parents, on the other hand, wrung out the surface appearance of rituals to show me how they functioned on a more symbolic level. When I asked about Santa Claus as a kid, my mother took several minutes to explain to me that while Santa Claus does appear once a year as a man who brings us gifts, he also exists all the time as the "spirit of love." And she said the spirit of love was also symbolized by the Christ child, and that it was in all of us, and it surrounded us. That's paganism, Christianity, Buddhism, and secular capitalism all in one.

At dinner, before eating, my parents had the four of us hold hands around the table and close our eyes in the manner of saying a prayer. But instead of speaking rote phrases to a specified divine being, my sister and I were told just to think about whatever we wanted. It was a moment of silence, like a mini meditation.

In an age when religion exists almost solely as the husks of once-rich practices, my parents sought for the lost layers. This seeking was their religion and, thus, the one they were passing down to me.

———

In preparation for my postaccident Ally meditations, I did some reading into shamanism and was relieved to find that, although talking to one's spirit guide is not exactly mainstream at the moment, there is a very long history—thousands of years—of people doing it. The only snag is, consistently, these people are considered to be insane.

The trembling shaman sent into an epileptic fit as he contacts the spirits is an old cliché. As it turns out, there is some truth in it. According to Romanian historian Mircea Eliade's book on shamanism, conditions in parts of the world where that practice thrived, such as the Arctic, were so severe—extreme cold, long nights, lack of vitamins—that the human nervous system was considerably damaged. This led to certain weaker individuals getting the shakes, having nervous breakdowns, or becoming epileptic. Without science to explain what was happening, the community assumed this person was being contacted by spirits, and conferred upon him or her the title of healer. Later, shamans would learn to create these conditions deliberately, with the goal of literally driving themselves insane. Starvation, going on a diet of tree bark only, throwing oneself into a fire or stabbing oneself with a knife—all these methods were used to obtain that shamanistic edge. Among the Tungus people of Asia, a would-be shaman took off to the mountains by himself for weeks, feeding only on animals killed by his own hands, returning to the village completely transformed—bloody, dirty, clothes torn and falling off his back. If he appeared crazy enough, the village accepted him as their shaman.

Then there are those who just sat back and were contacted by a spirit in a vision or a dream. People who hear voices are generally considered to be out of their minds, though history has a way of looking fondly on them. Moses and Jesus heard the word of God and translated it for all the average God-deaf folk. At the beginning of the fifteenth century Joan of Arc, only thirteen years old, famously heard a voice that she described as being from God, one that eventually instructed her to lead an insurrection in France, for which she was executed and became a martyr. These people didn't have to starve themselves, thrust knives into their chests, or put red ants in their pants to be visited by a spirit, God, or whatever they called it. They were contacted quite suddenly while going about their normal lives.

During his period of miniature village building and mandala scribbling, Jung would close his eyes and imagine himself on "a steep descent," going down as far as he could. One time, he said it felt as if he had found himself "at the edge of a cosmic abyss." In this darkness, he eventually landed on the moon and met fantastical figures, one of whom turned into the man he called Philemon. According to Jung, "Philemon was a pagan and brought with him an Egypto-Hellenistic atmosphere with a Gnostic coloration." He spoke to Philemon in his head and in his head Philemon would answer, saying things he had not consciously prompted, giving Jung guidance and what he called "superior insight." At one point, Jung asked Philemon how he could speak of ideas to Jung inside of Jung's head that Jung had not conceived himself. Philemon answered that thoughts were not always generated by the thinker. "If you should see people in a room," Philemon told Jung, "you would not think that you had made those people, or that you were responsible for them."

Jung concluded that "there are things in the psyche which I do not produce, but which produce themselves and have their own life." So, similar to his conclusion about mandalas, Jung considered this alien voice that came from within to be more evidence of the collective unconscious, that there are mytho-poetic materials in our psyches passed down from a mysterious historical source.

If Jung was crazy, he pulled off the biggest trick of all—using scientific-sounding psychobabble and creating a whole new system of thought to explain it.

As I researched all this, still in a post accident fog, I couldn't help thinking that shamans could still exist today and that maybe, just maybe, *I* was a shaman. Sure, I was just a guy living in Toronto, Canada, writing the odd book review, but maybe my real purpose was to heal the souls of my village. After all, I'd gone through the intense physical trauma of the bike accident, akin to the suffering shamans of yore put themselves through. And similar to, um, Jesus, I'd been visited by a spirit in my dream as a boy. (I may have been suffering temporarily from a delusional Messiah complex, but who doesn't at times?)

When I told my father about my research, he put me in touch with one of his colleagues who'd written a dissertation on people who were contacted by supernatural beings. He wrote that William Blake—the British Romantic poet whom I'd loved so much in university—had claimed to have been visited as a boy by God, whom he saw through his family's living room window. Inspired by this experience, Blake later wrote this line of poetry: "Then the divine Vision like a silent Sun / appeared above / Albions' dark rocks, setting behind the Gardens of Kensington."

Silent sun! It matched up exactly with the "shadowy sun" that I had seen in my dream. When I read in Eliade's book that one way a shaman can gain his healing knowledge and visionary profession is by inheriting it from his parents, I was hooked.

It was a dark and stormy night when I finally assumed the cross-legged position on the couch, my hands resting on my thighs, palms heavenward. If nothing else, the apocalyptic thunder outside would make the exercise feel suitably religious.

I geared myself up for what I call big listening. Small listening would be when you listen for sounds that occur in the objects around you: the rain on the street, the whistling wind, footsteps of the people living above. That's easy. The big listening challenge is to hear or see things—voices, sounds, colors, and images—from the *inside*. Inside your head. For people who have a psychotic disorder, the voices come to them unbidden and usually say pretty nasty things. But for me, hearing strange voices and having visions was something I'd learned to do from my parents. From a very young age, I had spent a lot of time closing my eyes and answering the questions, "Do you hear anything? Do you see anything?" Eventually, I'd see something, even if it was just a shape or shade of color passing beneath my eyelids.

"I see a purple line."

"Does the purple line have a name?"

"Purplehorn."

"Does it say anything?"

"It says, 'Ride me!'"

The idea is to use your imagination. Not in a creative way,

where you try to make up a meaning, but in a receptive, unconscious way, where you let the first thing that emerges from the
darkness in your head speak. Soon, you're flying on a six-legged
purple unicorn over New York City, and you don't know whether
you came up with that or if it always existed and simply emerged
into the world through your imagination.

I closed my eyes. First, it was just dark and I saw nothing. That
didn't surprise me, since my eyes were closed. A minute passed
very slowly, after which it was still dark, and I saw nothing. It's
weird, but I realized that holding my eyes shut was hard to do. I
was actually exerting my eyelid muscles quite a bit, which I worried would distract me from hearing the voice of my Ally, if it was
in fact going to say something.

"Ally, do you exist?" I asked.

No answer.

"Are you real? Who are you?"

I waited about half a minute, and as I was about to call out to
the Ally a third time, a bright flash of light passed before my eyes.
My heart started to pound and my stomach fell away. Holy shit, I
thought, this is it, and waited for the voice of the Ally to stream its
otherworldly poetry into my head. Then I heard the sound of tires
spraying up water on the wet street below and realized that the
flash was only the car's headlights coming through the window of
my apartment.

But I didn't give up. I carried on for half an hour or so, and
did this three times over the span of a week. I saw a lot of things,
certainly. I'm a storyteller after all, and I'd had a lot of practice

imagining dreamlike narratives. Plus, I really did want it to work.
I wanted to be a shaman. At least, my ego did.

Most remarkably, at one point I saw a flash of a figure—a bare-
chested man with reddish brown skin and the pointed mask of
an animal over his head. He was looking off to his right so that
I was seeing the mask in profile. It was the crude shape of a long
dog snout and large, pointed ears—one of those Egyptian figures
carved into the walls of cities thousands of years ago, that you see
now on slot machines in Las Vegas or have to hit your ball through
at a mini-golf course. I began to fear that my Ally was not actually
a sun but some clichéd Egyptian god. But then later there was a
flying dragon, circling and slithering around me, which looked
like a cheesy reproduction of an ancient painting on the wall of
a mall in Chinatown. Just how many trite images of deities were
lodged in my brain, I wondered. As it turns out, more. During my
last meditation, I saw an eagle and, then, perhaps inspired by my
rereading of Carlos Castaneda, I turned into an eagle myself and
started doing loop-de-loops in the sky.

Immediately after my last meditation, I decided to mimic what
my father had done with my Ally dream when I was a kid and
looked up some of these symbols. I was especially curious about
the eagle because I was sure it would be the pinnacle of animal
symbolism in ancient shamanism. The eagle, it turns out, is
known by the Buryat people of Tibet as "the bird of the sun," and
they believe he was sent down by God to bring the art of shamanistic healing to humans. Unfortunately, the eagle was speaking in
eaglish, so nobody on Earth could understand what he was saying.

Realizing his failure, God decided to try again. The second time, he sent the eagle down to have a different kind of communion. The eagle searched the planet until he found a young, beautiful woman sleeping under a tree. After what was likely a very strange seduction, they made love, and the child born from the union simply inherited the eagle's knowledge into his genes and became the first shaman.

I looked up the Egyptian figure from my first meditation and discovered that it was not a dog mask he wore, but a jackal's. The figure's name is Duamutef, one of the four sons of the Egyptian sun god Horus. According to Jung, similar to the Indian myth where Brahma looks in four directions before creation, the four sons of Horus represent the four cardinal directions as they extend out from the center of Horus, represented as a circle. The image created is a mandala, and identical to the picture I drew of my Ally dream when I was eight years old. And Duamutef, I learned, was the son who represented the east, the direction from which the sun rises!

The parallels between my original Ally dream, my mother's declaration that my Ally was a sun, and these meditations I'd done over twenty years later were astounding.

The high didn't last for long though. A week later, I didn't feel any different and my skepticism returned. Couldn't all the connections simply illustrate the fact that people will find connections wherever they want to? Given the millions of stories and myths from cultures around the world, how hard is it to find a connection between anything you can think of and the sun? Was a spirit guide speaking to me, or was I just flipping randomly through the photo album of humanity's collective memory?

. . .

Incidentally, during one of the meditations, I had also remembered that getting advice was one of the advantages of having an Ally. At one point I asked the void behind my eyelids about an issue of tantamount importance to me at the time.

"Can you help me," I called out, "write my book?"

Almost immediately, I had a vision of my head cracking down the middle, all the way to my brain, and falling apart into two halves. Then the image froze and turned to gray like the ash aftermath of a volcano.

I didn't take this as a very good sign. I opened my eyes, a bit dejected. Even the almighty Ally, I thought to myself, can't break through writer's block.

Shortly after I'd done the meditations, Beth and I were visiting her brother Dean, who at the time was a student of cognitive psychology. As we were preparing dinner, Dean and I got into a discussion about some topic relating to his studies, and I brought up one of Jung's philosophies, to which he responded, "Jung is considered irrelevant among today's thinkers." Beth overheard the conversation and leapt to the rescue: "Dean! Micah's parents are Jungians." Dean immediately apologized. I'd already heard this from my friend Helen and assured him I wasn't offended, but he was shy to elaborate on Jung's irrelevancy. Dean would only add that if you're doing cutting-edge research now, you no longer need to know Jung.

Later when we were alone, I told Dean about the concept of the Ally, about its role as a guiding spirit.

"That's very useful," he said after a pause, "and I would love to believe in something like that, but it can't be scientifically reconciled." Dean had once been the most religious person in his family—and had gone through his own delusional Messiah period—but he'd since become a reluctant atheist. "I *want* to believe in something," he said, "but my religious beliefs would have to be proven by science."

"But something like an Ally is so subjective," I said. "It could never be known by anyone else." He agreed that this might be the case, but until he reconciled those two things, he could only look at spirituality in terms of usefulness. He then surprised me by telling me that he recognized advice I'd given him in the past— about realizing that one's desire comes from within and thus can be reclaimed from all of the sexy women passing one by on the street—as coming from Jung, and that it had been really helpful to him. When he said that, a window of clarity opened up in my head. I'm not a shaman, I thought, *I'm a Jungian.* I possessed Jungian knowledge passed down to me from my parents, and used it to help me through hard times in my life. Unless I was to go through an extremely rigorous brainwashing and reconstruction of all my beliefs, that way of seeing things was something that made me who I am, and was affecting me in ways that I wasn't even aware of.

Although I couldn't prove it scientifically, all my parents' talk of my Ally and the "spirit of love" made me believe in something—I just wasn't able to pinpoint exactly what it was. Maybe that made me a spirit guide agnostic: I wasn't sure I really believed in the Ally, but I also didn't know that it doesn't exist.

In the meantime, I continued signing my name on birthday cards with a small sun next to it. *Just in case.*

———

A few weeks after I'd done the Ally meditations, I finally got around to talking to Beth about it. I told her what I'd seen: the Las Vegas Egyptian, the Chinatown dragon, and the episode I like to refer to as "I am the Bird-Man." I told her about some of the parallels between these visions and what Jung had written in his book on symbols. Like Jung had, I think I made it sound all very intelligent. I told her also about the debate going on in my head as to what it all meant for me, that I was still figuring out which parts of my parents' religion I was going to accept.

"Huh," she said, thinking about it. She seemed actually fascinated. "So are you hearing the voice of the Ally right now?" she asked.

"Wait a second, I think I do hear something," I said, pausing. "Something's wrong . . . I don't have a beer in my hand. My Ally is saying you should go get me one."

"Very funny. My Ally says you can kiss my ass."

8

Individuation

(The Elusive Conclusion)

"Micah," the minister said in his gravest tone of voice, "do you take Beth to be your lawfully wedded wife?"

It was the sunniest September afternoon I had ever seen. Just moments before, Beth had carefully made her way across the lawn in white high heels, holding on to her father's arm for her life. The cello's taut notes cut through the still air as the two of them took small steps toward the aisle. I stood waiting in front of sixty-five of our friends and family, my back to Lake Divine. The setting was near to Beth's heart, twenty minutes away from her family's cottage in northern Ontario where we spent many weekends in the summer and where I had bonded with what would become my new family.

When we made eye contact, Beth began to cry. My heart jumped at seeing my bride in her long white dress. Her father passed her over to me with a wink and then Beth and I stood facing each other in an extended mutual smile.

It's rare for someone as restless as I am to feel as if he is exactly where he is supposed to be in any moment, but that's how I felt as I stood there facing her. In front of everybody, and at this climactic moment in my life, I felt at peace.

The ceremony was fairly traditional, or as traditional as a Unitarian service can be. Our minister replaced "man" and "woman" in the service with nongendered terms so as not to alienate our homosexual guests, but he did insist on mentioning God several times. Beth and I had decided we were okay with this because God could mean whatever people wanted it to mean. It was a vague enough term to include the Ally, the green mist, or some gray-bearded authoritarian in the sky who—supposedly—didn't have a dark side. I wore a yellow tie as a tribute to my inner sun and Beth's ring had an emerald at its center.

Our minister paused and watched me after he had asked the crucial question. I waited a moment to let it sink in, to think about it and not just repeat automatically what I'd heard said in a hundred movies. I breathed in, I breathed out.

"I do," I said in my gravest tone of voice.

The minister turned to Beth.

"And Beth, do you take Micah to be your lawfully wedded wife?"

Beth opened her mouth but then froze.

"Um, you mean husband?" she said, bursting out laughing. Everyone else laughed as well. I rolled my eyes.

"Sorry!" the minister exclaimed, blushing. "Yes, I meant husband. Do you take Micah to be your husband? Sorry about that."

"It's okay," she said. "Yes, I do."

We kissed and after the crowd shouted "Bravo!" we kissed again. Then William put a lightbulb on the ground near me and I crushed it with my foot.

"Mazel Tov!" everyone exclaimed.

————————

The event of two opposites coming together became something of a big deal for Jung at the end of his life. By that point, he had developed an intricate theory to explain how the unconscious worked and the best practices by which one can bring more of it to awareness. He called the entire process *individuation*. Previously, the term had been used to describe an infant's psychic separation from his mother, but Jung had something else in mind.

"In general," he wrote of individuation, "it is the process by which individual beings are formed and differentiated; in particular, it is the development of the psychological individual as being distinct from the general, collective psychology."

Through the self-reflection inherent in analysis, Jung felt that a person could come to know who he is, separately and individually from all the various groups that he belongs—his country, his race, his species, and his family. You may think you know who you are already, but Jung felt you really didn't until you integrated your shadow, stopped projecting your inner feminine side or inner masculine side onto every woman or man you meet, and came to accept the totality of your identity without using other people's opinions as a crutch. The all-knowing individuated person doesn't just know who he *thinks* he is in any given moment—which is simply the view from the ego—but knows all that *and* knows all that is locked away in the darkness of his unconscious. Becoming individuated is the psychic equivalent of those times when you're cleaning your house and for some reason you get *really* into it, dusting every single surface, throwing away stuff that's been sitting around for years, and organizing every single object in every dark corner of every room. Don't worry, I haven't done that for a while either.

Individuation, it seems to me, is the same thing Buddhists seek in enlightenment. These days, it's what middle-class postreligious urban dwellers mean when they say, "I just want to be happy."

The idea is somewhat simple, but in the last twenty years of his life, Jung felt the need to come up with an extremely complicated explanation for it.

When Jung interpreted dreams, he liked to use mythology to show his clients that there was a precedent for the images that flowed through their heads at night. Their dreams, he thought, expressed archetypal remnants from the dreams of civilizations past, or else were simply echoes of those dreams since all dreams came from the same source. By comparing his client's dreams to the myths, Jung could use the stories as a discussion point to help his clients decide what to do next in the plots of their own lives. But over time, as he developed a complete picture of the pathway toward individuation, Jung became frustrated by the lack of a good myth to act as the metamyth, one that could explain the whole process of self-realization. Then, in the late 1920s, Jung started reading about the ancient practice of alchemy and realized he'd struck gold.

I'd heard of alchemy as a kid—alchemists turned things into gold, which, even back then, I knew to be impossible. I always pictured a bunch of guys hundreds of years ago playing with beakers in their garages, blowing things up, their faces turning black. According to Jung, that portrait I got from Saturday morning television cartoons is not the full picture.

Jung spent decades collecting European alchemical texts dating as far back as the fifteenth century, meticulously translating and decoding them and then describing the parallels between the alchemical process and the path to individuation. His last major work on the topic, *Mysterium Coniunctionis*, a massive tome of over six hundred pages, outlines his conclusions. It is Jung's *Ulysses*, Jung's *Infinite Jest*, drawing allusions from hundreds of sources, and, like those sources, is nearly unreadable but to a committed few.

Alchemists, Jung decided, were not just protochemists messing around in a laboratory, they were more like metaphysical philosophers. They had grand abstract ideas about how consciousness worked but knew very little about how matter came into being. So they took their philosophical ideas about the human spirit and applied them to the minerals they cooked in their beakers.

According to Marie-Louise von Franz, Jung's steadfast assistant in his quest to solve the code of this ancient practice, alchemists writing in Greek even sometimes used the same word for metaphysical concepts and the concrete matter they used in their formulas. "For instance," she writes, "sulphur is called *theion*, which also means divine." This caused great confusion for both von Franz and Jung, because they never knew in each instance how to correctly translate such words and, consequently, didn't know whether any given text was a philosophical treatise or a recipe for gold. Jung decided finally that it was both.

Coniunctio is the Latin term for the union of two opposite things. In one of Jung's books on alchemy, he reproduces the drawings alchemists created to illustrate the concept and, perhaps not surprisingly, most of them are of people having sex. The gist of the connection between alchemy and Jung's path to individuation, if I may humbly reduce decades of work and writing down to one idea, is that if properly "cooked"—either in the beakers or in therapy, depending on whether you're talking about matter or an individual's psyche—two things of opposite natures can create the birth of something new.

The alchemists sometimes referred to the process as the "chymical marriage." The union can happen at many different levels—countries, cities, two people—but Jung was especially interested in the union that occurs inside the individual psyche. We are all full of contradictions, Jung thought, and instead of just brushing that aside, therapy could help a person unite them, bringing about a greater awareness and, possibly, individuation.

———————

"Your parents can't do therapy with you," my friend Helen told me a few years ago when I suggested I didn't need to see a therapist because I could always just talk to my parents about my problems.

"Well, I know it's not exactly therapy, but they can teach me some of the tools that I can then use on my own, so I don't really need a therapist."

"You don't understand," she would say, shaking her head. "*They* are part of your problems. You have to talk to someone about *them*."

"I don't have any problems with *them*," I said.

"Well, you don't think you do."

For most of my life, I'd gotten along with my parents almost without any conflicts. When I lived with my father after the divorce we had ongoing disagreements about household chores, but our fights never went much beyond these practical matters. My mother and I seemed never to argue, a fact that I once did find suspicious, but when I brought it up to her as a possible problem she told me not to worry about it.

The Jungian practices that my mother and father taught me were all in the great effort to individuate me, to make me more conscious, to bring about my own chemical transformation into a healthy adult. What was wrong with that? And after all, I had succeeded in finding a wife and my wedding was a rite of passage that proved I had created my own individuality, was breaking away from my family, combining with an "opposite" and starting my own family. My father—not one to overlook Jung even in a wedding speech—explained to all of our guests that I was following the path of the hero as outlined in Joseph Campbell's *The Hero with a Thousand Faces,* the book that inspired *Star Wars* and which goes through the individuation process step by step as seen in myths from time immemorial.

"Part of the hero's process," he lectured to our family and friends, "is that he forges a new life of his own." My marriage, he pointed out, was the beginning of that.

It was true: from ideas I learned from my parents, I had started to integrate my shadow, was trying not to project my anima, was taking cues from my dreams, and, most important at this stage, I was no longer using my parents as a psychic crutch.

Well, maybe I hadn't quite mastered that last one.

"She tells me that I should finish off the old tomato before cutting into a new one, and I guess I know what she means. She just makes such a big deal about it!"

I was talking on the phone out of hearing distance from Beth. This was years before our wedding, when we were twenty-three and had just begun living together. We were going to battle over extremely important domestic arrangements.

"And what do *you* want to do?" my mother asked me.

"I don't know. I mean, I know that we would be better off if I finished the old tomato. That's the best thing to do economically and ecologically. But I just feel like cutting into the new tomato. The old one is soggy."

"So then that's what you need to say—I feel like cutting into the new tomato! Remember when we did that process where you

became the Incredible Hulk and you were unstoppable? You need
to be that."

"Okay," I said, feeling inspired.

I remembered the process she was talking about, another one
we had done in a public park, this time in New York, where, relative to Boulder, Colorado, we probably didn't look as crazy.

But, after I hung up with my mother, I did not become the
Incredible Hulk. I did not tell Beth, using an exclamation point,
that I was going to cut into the new tomato whether she liked
it or not. I may have mumbled something about choosing personal enjoyment in life over what was supposedly the right thing
to do, but soon I was following the refrigerator rules as dictated
by Beth.

Whenever I called my mother about interpersonal problems I
was having, she could usually help me feel better, even if I never
ended up actually standing my ground. She would use the knowledge she'd learned from her psychological training and experience to steer me through my frustration. And, best—or worst—of
all, she had a knack for turning things around so that I would
appear in the right.

Years later, when Beth realized that I sometimes still brought
my issues to my mother—though, in my defense, it had become
less frequent and rarely included vegetables—she was not super
psyched about it. The issue finally came to a head after my bicycle
accident.

A couple months after I'd returned from the hospital, my mother
wanted to visit, in part because the purpose of her latest pet psy-

chological technique—which she called "trauma work"—was to
help clients overcome things like near-death bike accidents. She
booked her trip for eight days and told me this would give us just
enough time to work through some of the psychological scarring
that had occurred.

"That's a long visit," Beth said when I told her.

"It's not that long," I replied. "She lives so far away and I never
see her."

"All I said was that it is a long visit."

"I know what you're implying. Anyway, I couldn't tell her to
come for less time."

"Why?"

"Because she said it'll take that much time to work through the
trauma. And, I just can't say that to her. I can't tell her I'd rather
she leave earlier."

"Micah, you have to be able to be honest with her. It's not
healthy to just do whatever she wants. And," she said, gaining
steam, "it's not okay for you to be doing therapy with her!"

"I don't do therapy with her!" I shouted. "You don't understand, her method is not Freudian where I tell her every little
thing about my sex life. Okay, *yes,* I once or twice did do that, but
I don't anymore. She's just going to have me meditate on the ways
I was feeling when I was hit by the car."

"Well, whatever. I'm just saying, relying on your mother like
that doesn't help in the long run—it's what causes anxiety. That's
not something I just came up with, people have been saying that
forever." It was funny being psychoanalyzed by Beth. She didn't
know nearly as much about the analytical process as my mother
or I did. And yet, she had a point.

"You should go see someone else," she insisted, and not for the first time.

During my mother's visit, for a couple hours each day, she taught me how to do the meditation. I'd sit completely still while describing in detail the things that were going through my mind during each tiny moment of the accident. Essentially, the purpose of this was to resolve each moment of horror through consciously becoming aware of it. My mother felt that trauma could only stay in you and keep affecting you if you ignored and repressed it. One of the more surprising suggestions she made was that I take an extreme bicycle acrobatics course and learn how to do jumping tricks or else leap off of my bike at a moment's notice. She said that if my body knew how to respond next time a car comes flying through a red light toward me, not only might I be able to avoid another impact, but, more important, my body would be freed of its sense of helplessness and so wouldn't keep experiencing the trauma every time I got back on a bike.

I consider doing this type of exercise with my mother harmless. Still, Beth and Helen both had their fingers on the reason why a parent can't and shouldn't play psychic mediator for her child—a little problem called transference.

I'm a big fan of the actress Naomi Watts. Aside from the fact that she makes excellent role choices and has worked with several of my favorite directors, I just have a huge crush on her. Since I don't know her at all, I suppose this means she represents an aspect of my anima that I need to learn to embody. Anyway, she made a small-budget and remarkably meta film once about being an actress looking for work and going through a comical nervous breakdown. During the course of the film, she goes to a couple therapy sessions, and at one point is talking to a guy she meets about her therapist.

"You want to know something really weird?" she says.

"Yeah."

"My therapist has a crush on me."

He laughs. "That's kind of, um, what's supposed to happen a little bit. It's called transference."

"Yeah, transference. I know. But this is not that. This is seriously awkward. I feel like she's undressing me right there on the couch. And every time I'm about to leave, I walk away and I think I'm going to feel good and then she has to say something negative, as if to say, come back. Love me, love me, love me, love me. Need me, need me, need me, need me."

At an early point in the therapeutic process, the client is supposed to fall in love with the therapist, or at least form a very strong connection to him or her. The theory is that the client—let's say he's a man seeing a woman—is substituting his therapist for his mother. Or, in Jungian terms: he projects his mother onto his therapist. The duty of the therapist is then to use the transference to re-create that relationship in therapy and, hopefully, through a mediated version of it, get the client to resolve issues embedded since childhood. Since the therapist is not actually the client's mother, she has the perspective to step out of that role and point out to the client his unhealthy behavior and thus help him own up to his own shit.

"Once the projections are recognized as such," writes Jung, "the particular form of rapport known as transference is at an end, and the problem of individual relationship begins." That is, if both of them can get past the parent-child baggage, then the work of helping the client find his individual path can start.

Freud was also concerned about something he called counter-transference, wherein the therapist believes the patient has really fallen in love with him or her. The therapist, he wrote, "must recognize that the patient's falling in love is induced by the analytic situation and is not to be attributed to the charms of his own person; so that he has no grounds whatever for being proud of such a 'conquest', as it would be called outside analysis."

To give an example of just how complicated transference can sometimes get, in the film scene I described above with Naomi Watts, despite what the guy says, she seems to be actually describing countertransference as opposed to transference. But, since it is a countertransference seen from the client's point of view, my analysis would be that she experiences her transference as an imagined countertransference.

––––––––––

Recently, when my father found out that my mother and I had been in the habit of discussing my personal problems, as well as doing some processes together, he became concerned. He came across this fact in the detailed outline of this book, which I sent to him. I thought he might be upset about some of what I was going to write, but I hadn't foreseen that the synopsis would be the catalyst for my parents' reunion after all these years.

My father called my mother and warned her that there was a danger, if it hadn't happened already, of my becoming "enmeshed," a psychological term that means what it sounds like—a disorder of an adult being too tangled up emotionally with a parent. He didn't warn me he was going to make the call—I learned about it when, afterward, my mother called me in something of a panic.

"Do you think that I messed you up?" she asked me.

"Uh, what?" I replied.

"Do you think us doing processes together messed you up psychologically?"

"Well, no," I said in as calm a voice as is possible in the face of one's parents' cooperatively—and okay, unintentionally—planting a seed of paranoia about the state of one's psyche. "For starters, I'm not messed up."

At that point, I'd already stopped calling her whenever a problem came up in my life. And after Beth had insisted that I be more honest with my mother and talk to a therapist who was not my parent, I had given a lot of thought to creating even firmer boundaries.

"I think it's possible that I have relied too much on you sometimes," I told her. "Because of your psychological knowledge and skills, I may have trusted your opinion about things too much and not thought enough on my own."

It was not an easy thing to say to her. Our bonding ever since my parents' divorce had been founded on discussing my issues.

"I'll still tell you about my life," I told her. "But you don't need to feel like you have to be the one to fix my problems."

She agreed with my analysis and prescription. The exchange felt exceedingly adultlike.

―――――――――

Jungians are usually required to go through their own therapy before they can be licensed to practice on innocent civilians so I felt a similar dialogue with my own psyche might be useful before writing about my parents' being shrinks.

My father speculated that the reason I had never gone to a therapist before was that I was repressing a distrust of psychologists, or else that I feared them. I always felt that it was laziness that stopped me. I was busy writing. I was busy at work. I was busy getting a drink with friends. I was busy watching television. I was busy staring at the wall in a fit of anxiety over something, occasionally slipping into psychic meltdowns.

When the hour of my first session arrived, it was odd not to be sitting in a waiting room like the one my father had in our house. The chair in the strange building wasn't cushy like all my father's chairs and, instead of being alone, I was sitting next to a man who was also waiting for his therapist. I wondered what was wrong with him and whether I was allowed to ask. When a couple more people came in and filled all the available seats, my mind wandered to the pervasiveness of this thing we called therapy. In the four-storied building in which I sat, a therapy emporium, there were probably about twenty people sitting across from therapists, confessing their deepest secrets, narrating their romantic dilemmas. And this, I thought, is only one office building in one city in a world that's filled with psychologists. Hundreds, thousands, *tens* of thousands of people were partaking in the same ritual at any given moment, and in that same moment. Together, we formed an army of self-reflection, a human-powered engine burrowing into the collective unconscious.

We were talking about our mothers and fathers. We were describing dreams in which our teeth fall out or we are back in school but wearing no clothes. We were asserting that we could have been more loved or that we weren't allowed to be angry. And how we are angry now. Or not angry, but depressed. We are anxious. We are an army of depressive anger and angry anxiety and anxious depression.

When I was called in to meet my very own therapist, the experience again was strangely unfamiliar. I had imagined somehow that I would be sitting across from a combination of my parents. But here was this woman who looked nothing like my mother or, thankfully, my father.

From the beginning, I wanted to be a difficult case. I wanted my therapist to feel as if she were being challenged, taken to the limits of her psychotherapeutic powers. I wanted her to have her mind blown by my psyche.

I'm not supposed to share with the general populace the intimate details of my therapy sessions—doing so, I was told, would threaten to infect the process—but I will say that it was an impressive performance on my part. After I left my first session, I was chuffed, thinking that indeed I had presented my brilliant mind well. I would certainly be the central focus of my therapist's future book about the complex psychology of the modern intellectual.

That was before I read the following passage in Jung's memoir: "The spirit does not dwell in concepts, but in deeds and in facts. Words butter no parsnips. . . . In my experience, therefore, the most difficult as well as the most ungrateful patients, apart from habitual liars, are the so-called intellectuals."

Rather than being someone my therapist looked forward to seeing all week long, was I that annoying, overly analytical person who thinks so much that it's impossible to get at what's going on with him? Maybe. I'd at least try to be grateful, even though I'm the one paying.

When I told my parents I was seeing a therapist, I felt like I was betraying them—as if I were saying that they weren't good enough.

"What *kind* of therapist is she?" my father asked.

I had purposefully not gone to a Jungian.

"I don't know," I lied. "I got a referral from a friend." The truth is, I realized that I had trusted the opinions of my parents about my psychic development too exclusively. Their expertise in the area caused me to sometimes consider them all-knowing about my own mind and emotions. Seeing a therapist was me striking off into my own individual psychological frontiers, and my first rebellion down that path was not seeing a Jungian.

My therapist described her method as "psycho-dynamic," which I had never heard of. When I finally told my father this, he translated it as "refined Freudianism." Given the feud that remains between Freudians and Jungians, this was a suitably potent act of psychological rebellion.

––––––––

People usually assume that my psychologist parents would have messed with my head, but it seems to me that all parents, regardless of profession, mess with their kids' heads. For instance, a mother doesn't have to be a therapist to smother a child or be a controlling presence in her son's life. A father doesn't have to be a shrink for a kid to feel like he's being judged for living a life his father doesn't approve of. My parents' being psychologists only changed the language of it.

And the fact is, a mother can't do real therapy with her son. See, the transference wouldn't work. I already *do* have a bond with my mother and I can't substitute her for my mother because she already is my mother. In my case, when my mother used her therapeutic knowledge to help me with issues, the part that got in the way was that I wanted to please her. I wanted it to work for her sake as well as mine. So I sometimes lied, even if unconsciously, so that things would seem to come out fine in the end. Now, I may want to do the same thing with my current therapist, who is not my mother, but it's her duty to be able to use that projection to challenge me in a way that my mother can't.

For instance, in my first therapy session, I was annoyed that my therapist wouldn't laugh at any of my jokes. They were hilarious jokes! When I told her at the end of the session that I wasn't sure I was going to come back because it seemed like she didn't "get" me, she responded with the challenge: "Why do you need me to like you?" Well, that opened up a month's worth of work right there. She earned herself a few hundred dollars from that one question. But imagine my mother saying something like that to me. She never could.

In fact, I wouldn't even want my mother to be able to detach herself so much from being my mother that she would be able to tell me in what way I should and should not be attached to her. And if she did, it only gives birth to this mind-bending paradox: If your mother is telling you that you need to be more independent from her, then in the end, if you follow that advice, you would be doing so because she said to do it. That's no way to become individuated.

These days, the various Jungian policing bodies consider doing therapy with your family members a breach of their code of ethics, but this was not always the case. Jung's solution to dealing with his wife's jealousies over his rumored affairs was to analyze her. And back in the early days, everybody was analyzing everybody. "No boundaries had yet been defined; there were no rules, no standards of behavior," Jung's biographer Deirdre Bair concluded after interviewing and reading the journals of the people in the scene at that time. "Therapists were often teachers, friends, or lovers of their patients; socializing and entertainment existed in tandem with therapeutic treatment; massive egos frequently collided, as theoreticians sought dominance for pet theories and sometimes even pet analysands."

I remember a similar scene around my parents in the early 1980s. Both my mother and father had sessions with a therapist who was their friend and whose family we shared Thanksgiving with each year. He and his wife had kids the same age as my sister and me. My father was also his therapist's racquetball partner. Ally meditations never came up over turkey, but there was the odd Jungian joke cracked. I once announced to them all, out of nowhere, while eating dinner: "I have a sun complex. I'm burning up!" That produced the loudest laugh of the evening and I beamed with pride that I had said something so psychologically clever.

I wonder on the whole why Jungians now feel they have so much to worry about. Certainly a Freudian-trained mother would not want to ask her son if he remembers the first time he saw her naked and how he felt about that, but a Jungian mother wouldn't run into the same problems comparing his dream about flying into the sun, say, to an Icarus myth. It's true that Jungian therapists sometimes talk to their clients about early family life, but they can also choose the more esoteric route, one that I would think leads less to enmeshment.

One thing is certain, though. When the child of Jungians makes his move to individuate, his parents will be uniquely aware of it.

————————

During a recent trip home during Christmas, I stayed at the house my father shared with his soon-to-be third wife. The three of us got into a discussion about familial rebellion.

My father told me that when he had decided to marry my mother, his stepfather tried to convince him not to, insisting that it was a terrible decision to get involved with the needy single mother of a black child. His stepfather even tried to bribe him to leave her, a fact that astounded me. Talk about overstepping boundaries! My father was equally disgusted and for some time didn't speak to his stepfather. I was proud of him for standing his ground.

"So, Micah," my father's girlfriend asked me, "have you ever rebelled?" She asked me this in a slightly skeptical tone, which she was right to do, since I'd always been so obedient.

"Well, I suppose that's what I'm doing now," I said.

I knew from the beginning that my father would not be happy about my writing a book about him and our family. Early on, I even hid my intentions from him, waiting until I had developed the idea more and had a publisher on board. For better or worse, the extreme frankness and regular confession that I was raised with made it so I couldn't keep a secret very long from anybody. If my heart and mind were not completely open books to those I was close to, I felt I was committing some sin of the collective unconscious, which is why I had finally sent him the outline.

I was correct in assuming he would not be happy about it. He didn't want events from his life put on display, and although he didn't put it this way exactly, I got the impression he didn't want me to have control over his persona. He's a private person and had no idea what I intended to write about, so he was understandably unsettled. Who wants the details of their family melodrama displayed for the public? Apparently, I do, but then I'm the one who gets to tell the story.

"I'm afraid if you write this book, you'll be unconsciously expressing your shadow," my father told me.

"But it's a lighthearted portrayal," I answered. "A lot of it is just meant to be funny."

"Humor is how the unconscious shadow comes out," he informed me.

"Well, how can anyone write anything if they're always worried about expressing their unconscious?" I replied. "That's often the whole point of writing."

"But it could be harmful."

"Maybe I'm just individuating," I said. "And that's why you're upset."

"That's true," he agreed. Briefly, I thought maybe I'd won. "But there are less destructive ways to individuate."

We went on like this, lobbing Jungian terms back and forth. By the end of the conversation, he had dropped the logical argument and had become emotional with me, which was rare for him. He was far more hurt than I thought he was going to be and he suggested that my book might break us.

When I got off the phone, I sat down on the living room couch and started to cry. It occurred to me that of course my father would say I should be less destructive as I individuated. That's what the individuatee—that is, the one being individuated against—would always say. I laughed a little, cursing the fact that the best comebacks always come to mind after the fact. I wondered, too, if it was now my turn to become the terrorist of the family.

"I don't think I can write my book," I told Beth when she came into the room. I explained to her what had happened, and although she understood my father's concern—after all, she too was nervous about being written about—she suggested I shouldn't react so abruptly.

"Give it time," she said. "Just keep writing and keep talking it out with him." After some time, I realized she was right and was once again impressed by her counseling skills.

As I continued on with my project despite my father's disapproval, at times I couldn't have asked for a better guide through it than Jung. Growing up, I was intrigued by his ideas, but I also wanted to look at him critically. Sometimes, though, as I delved into his writing, I found myself going native, suffering from a kind of Stockholm syndrome, using Jungian philosophy itself as a form of self-help, especially as it concerned shoring up the strength to go on in the face of filial disagreement.

In his memoir, Jung admits that people need to be members of groups. It makes them feel they belong and gives them a sense of identity. However, eventually you have to leave the safe haven of the collective and go on your own adventures.

"The secret society is an intermediary stage on the way to individuation," he wrote. "The individual is still relying on a collective organization to effect his differentiation for him; that is, he has not yet recognized that it is really the individual's task to differentiate himself from all the others and stand on his own feet. All collective identities, such as membership in organizations, support of 'isms,' and so on, interfere with the fulfillment of this task."

Jung admitted that this was easier said than done. "For the

most part, these sallies into no man's land last only as long as no such conflicts occur, and come swiftly to an end as soon as conflict is sniffed from afar. I cannot blame the person who takes to his heels at once. But neither can I approve his finding merit in his weakness and cowardice. Since my contempt can do him no further harm, I may as well say that I find nothing praiseworthy about such capitulations."

As it applies to one's family, Jung cautioned that one should individuate from his parents without causing too much of a rupture in the relationship. By writing about my parents, I worried that I was stepping over that line. But how was I supposed to know for sure? Jung doesn't have an answer to that because it's a question each person ultimately has to answer for himself. Jung does, however, offer many a rallying cry in support of the uncertain endeavor.

"Anyone who takes the sure road is as good as dead," he wrote, a drama queen after my own heart.

Reaching a permanent individuated state is not a realistic goal. An argument could be made that there is only one known case of this ever occurring: Buddha. And who knows how much of that was just him posing—it's easy to appear a fully realized consciousness if you're just sitting under a tree.

You can integrate your inner badass and get cozy with your anima, but ultimately, life is just an endless series of challenging new situations against which you must repeatedly form your identity.

"The serious problems in life are never fully solved," writes Jung. "If ever they should appear to be so it is a sure sign that something has been lost. The meaning and purpose of a problem seem to lie not in its solution but in our working at it incessantly."

In the introduction to one of the books on alchemy that Marie-Louise von Franz wrote after Jung's death, she talks about the challenges that alchemists toiled under: they worked in hidden shacks in the woods for fear of being caught and persecuted as black magicians; they had to pay off local law enforcement; they were constantly harassed by greedy rulers who wanted the alchemists to make them some gold; and, last, they could be cooking together two minerals for days only to be thwarted by the heat going out before the transformation of materials was completed.

"See that your fire never goes out . . . otherwise you can start again," von Franz translated from one alchemist's diary.

It's an apt metaphor for marriage, too, where the fire doesn't always stay.

"My father's wedding is that same day," I told William recently over the phone, explaining why I couldn't be in New York for his birthday.

"He's marrying again? Wow, that man really has a lot of faith, doesn't he?"

I laughed. "Yeah, he just keeps going back for more."

It was my father's third marriage, a number that finally matched my mother's feat. Meanwhile, the woman my father was marrying was also on her third and my mother is Peter's fourth wife. Yes, I come from a long line of serial individuators.

This inability to maintain a sense of stasis in a relationship reminds me of the story my father told me about the time he went to an Arny seminar after having not attended one for a while: "I asked him how the last couple years had been for him and he said, 'Fantastic! I came down with a serious illness and then went through a divorce.' "

Arny, it seemed, thought that any bad thing that happened to you was good. In his books, he brings up death often and in the same counterintuitive spirit, he says that death can be the key to health. While discussing the death fantasies and dreams of his clients, he concludes at one point, "In my experience most of these fantasies try to create radical changes in life at a time when the ego feels blocked against the apparently inflexible forces of the world." The end of things, he seemed to be suggesting, is one of the greatest sources of learning about ourselves.

In Jung's memoir, he talks about a similar insight involving a literal death, that of his mother. The night she died, Jung had a dream that something he referred to as the "Wild Huntsman" commanded a "gigantic wolfhound" to "carry away a human soul." In the morning, he awoke to the news that his mother had passed away.

Jung was devastated with the loss and angry with the Wild Huntsman: "[D]eath is indeed a fearful piece of brutality; there is no sense pretending otherwise. It is brutal not only as a physical event, but far more so psychically: a human being is torn away from us, and what remains is the icy stillness of death. There no longer exists any hope of a relationship, for all the bridges have been smashed at one blow. Those who deserve a long life are cut off in the prime of their years, and good-for-nothings live to a ripe old age. This is a cruel reality which we have no right to sidestep. The actual experience of the cruelty and wantonness of death can so embitter us that we conclude there is no merciful God, no justice, and no kindness."

It's fairly depressing stuff, but once he'd collected himself, Jung, ever the optimist, also saw the glass as half full. He researched into the Wild Huntsman to remind himself of this mythological figure that had appeared in his dream and realized that his purpose was not an evil one. In Norse legends, the Wild Huntsman was synonymous with Mercury or Hermes, nature spirits that returned life to the earth.

"From another point of view, however, death appears as a joyful event," Jung wrote. "In the light of eternity, it is a wedding, a *mysterium coniunctionis*. The soul attains, as it were, its missing half, it achieves wholeness."

————

Years ago, a friend of mine was in the middle of telling me about the various ways that her parents—neither of them therapists, I should mention—had messed with her head. In the middle of her rant, she broke off suddenly and shouted, "They fuck you up, your mum and dad!"

"Geez, was it really that bad?" I asked.

She laughed. "That's not mine . . . it's the first line of a Philip Larkin poem."

She told me the whole poem is about the inevitability of this fact, that's there's no way around it, and the best thing you can do is not make the same mistake by having your own children.

Parents do indeed fuck you up. But it has occurred to me as an aspiring individuator that this *is* their job. If they don't fuck you up, they are failing as parents. I don't mean that parents should be abusive or deliberately screw with their kids' heads. But how is one supposed to burst forth as an individual if one has nothing to burst forth from? Our parents fucking us up is a time-honored catalyst for individuation.

At some point, though, one needs to get past the point of blaming one's parents for fucking one up. Yes, you've graduated from the Oedipus complex and now both your parents look like frail idiots. Way to go. Certainly, you must look down on them for a little while to rise up to their stature, but to view yourself as a differentiated person from your parents, I'd say you have to be able to step back and realize their flaws don't have so much to do with you. They are going through their own individuating, with all the struggles that entails.

It's been easier for me, as of late, to see things from that point of view, due to some time spent walking in their shoes. After ten years together, and three years after our wedding, Beth and I realized somewhat suddenly that our own "chymical marriage" was no longer golden.

After Beth and I separated and I'd been living alone in a bachelor apartment already for six months, we had dinner one evening to reflect on what had happened and what was going to happen.

We met at a nice Italian restaurant and chatted about our jobs, about our friends. We drank wine and made each other laugh. We talked a bit about what went wrong but still hadn't really figured it out. We arranged yet another date in the seemingly endless ordeal of separating our things. Finally, there was a lull in the conversation. Beth took a drink of wine and set her glass down carefully.

"I hope that you don't regret that you ever got together with me," she said.

I laughed. The idea of trying to take back ten years all at once seemed absurd. "Of course not," I said. "I don't even know how you could think that."

"Well, okay. I was just sad to think you might say something like that in your book. I don't regret it."

We looked each other in the eyes for a bittersweet moment.

"After all this and no matter what happens," she said, "our wedding day is still one of the happiest days of my life."

"Mine too," I agreed.

A year after the break up with Beth—the point at which our *coniunctio* was definitely going to become an un-*coniunctio*—my mother and I were talking about how nice the wedding had been and that it was too bad things had not worked out.

"Well, I guess we know now what it meant that your minister dropped your ring," she said. "And the fact that you got lost."

The morning of the wedding, I went off into the woods with some friends to take my last walk as an unmarried man. It was meant to be a short, casual stroll, but turned into a three-hour tour. The map we were given at the resort's front desk showed that the path would eventually circle back to the beginning, but the longer we walked, the more certain we were that we had made a wrong turn. At one point, half-crazy, I began sprinting down the path, only to collapse, breathless and lost. I spent precious minutes trying to calculate our position according to the sun, which was impossible since I'm not a tracker. I kept envisioning Beth walking down the aisle to nobody and the helicopters that would be hired to find us, as if the wedding wasn't already costing her parents enough.

"Why don't we just trace our way back the way we came," one of my friends said finally. We hadn't paid attention to all the twists and turns we'd made, so I didn't know if we'd just get more lost, but my friend said it with enough confidence to convince me it was worth a shot. Using landmarks and carefully retracing our steps, we did manage to find our way back, just in time for me to clean up and quickly make my way to the minister's side.

I had made it and the ceremony was going smoothly until my ring slipped out of the minister's hand and fell into the long grass. Even though I didn't see where it went, I knelt down and miraculously found it right away so that the wedding could proceed.

But were these events a sign that the marriage shouldn't happen? Was the universe synchronistically answering the question,

"Does anyone here have any reason that these two should not be wed?" Were Zeus and Hera—the god and goddess of the marriage archetype—trying to stop it? That's what my mother was suggesting.

"I don't know," I said. "I mean, couldn't it be equally true that since I got back in time and recovered the ring from the ground, it meant that I'd always be able to find a solution?"

I told her that, anyway, I was individuating now and I didn't need her to interpret symbols to tell me what was going right or wrong in my life. I could figure that out myself. She thanked me for correcting her.

"You're right," she said. "I was being too Freudian."

Acknowledgments

Many thanks to: My agent and great lunch date Doug Stewart and his assistant Seth Fishman; my excellent shrink, er, I mean, editor Alane Mason, her assistant Denise Scarfi, and everyone else who worked on this book at W. W. Norton; Kristin Cochrane, Tim Rostron, Martha Leonard, and the rest of the team at Doubleday Canada; Melanie Morassutti, Derek Finkle, Pat Lynch, and all of my former *Toro*mates. For their invaluable advice and support, thank you to: Jeff Warren, Toby Warren, the Warren folks, Jean Kaluk, Glen Fogel, Chris Longfellow, Brett Ogin, Damian Tarnopolsky, Seth Poulin, Lisan Jutras, Scott Anderson, Matthew Fox, Julie Devaney, Hollay Ghadery, Mark Schofield, and Jia Lu. Thank you to the Ontario Arts Council for their financial support. A special thanks to Jane Warren for her encouragement, understanding, and words of wisdom through it all, and to my writing ally Kelly Dignan. And, of course, this book would certainly not have been possible without my family—thanks, Dad, Mom, Eric, Kathy, Andreya, Christian, Fiona, and Jasmin.

Notes

Note on Sources

The source that I draw from more than any other for this book is *Memories, Dreams, Reflections* (Pantheon Books, 1965), C. G. Jung's posthumously published memoir. *MDR* was partly written by Jung himself and partly dictated to Aniela Jaffé, who also edited the text. For convenience, I've referred to Jung as having "written" the book throughout. All quotations and descriptions of Jung's life and ideas come from *MDR* unless otherwise referenced in the text or noted below. Many thanks to Random House, Inc., for granting me permission to excerpt from this invaluable source.

I list these notes in order of their appearance in each chapter unless I used a source more than once in a chapter, in which case I grouped the notes together when the source first appears.

Chapter 1. The Marginalized

Explanation of Arnold Mindell's worldwork conflict resolution practices and excerpts on "rejection of unmediated anger" by the mainstream: see Arnold Mindell, *Sitting in the Fire: Large Group Transformation Using Conflict and Diversity* (Lao Tse Press, 1995).

C. G. Jung excerpt on sibling rivalry: see C. G. Jung, *The Development of Personality* (Princeton University Press/Bollingen Foundation, 1954).

Explanation of Jung's "Jungfrauen" and C. G. Jung quotation on his "eternal line of spinsters": see Deirdre Bair, *Jung: A Biography* (Little Brown, 2003).

Description of Arnold Mindell's introduction to Jungian psychology and creation of Process-oriented psychology: see Arnold Mindell, *Quantum Mind* (Lao Tse Press, 2000).

Chapter 2. Dreambody

Description and excerpts throughout this chapter regarding Arnold Mindell's concept of the dreambody: see Arnold Mindell, *Dreambody: The Body's Role in Revealing the Self* (Sigo Press, 1982); and Arnold Mindell, *The Quantum Mind and Healing: How to Listen and Respond to Your Body's Symptoms* (Hampton Roads Publishing Company, Inc., 2004).

Chapter 3. The Oedipus Complex

Sigmund Freud excerpt on the "original consummation"; explanation of latency period and "re-finding" the love object: see Peter Gay, ed., "Three Essays on the Theory of Sexuality," in *The Freud Reader* (W. W. Norton, 1989).

Sigmund Freud excerpts describing and analyzing Oedipus myth: see Sigmund Freud, *Introductory Lectures on Psychoanalysis* (The Institute of Psycho-Analysis, 1963).

Excerpts from letters between Sigmund Freud and C. G. Jung regarding sexual nature of hysteria: see William McGuire, ed., *The Freud/Jung Letters: Abridged Edition* (Princeton University Press, 1974).

Sigmund Freud excerpt regarding "small lover": see Peter Gay, ed., "The Dissolution of the Oedipus Complex," in *The Freud Reader* (W. W. Norton, 1989).

C. G. Jung excerpts and description of his homosexual client: see C. G. Jung, *The Development of Personality* (Princeton University Press, 1954).

C. G. Jung quotation regarding Germany's Oedipus complex: see William McGuire and R.F.C. Hull, eds., *C. G. Jung Speaking: Interviews and Encounters* (Princeton University Press, 1977).

C. G. Jung excerpt regarding Oedipus complex causing "neurotic disturbances": see C. G. Jung, *Freud and Psychoanalysis* (Princeton University Press/Bollingen Foundation, 1961).

Description of Freud's relationship with daughter Anna: see Peter Gay, *Freud: A Life for Our Time* (W. W. Norton, 1988).

Description and excerpts regarding Jung's relationship with daughter Marianne: see Deirdre Bair, *Jung: A Biography* (Little Brown, 2003).

Chapter 4. Anima

Overview and excerpts of Jung's concept of the anima: see C. G. Jung, *Aion: Researches into the Phenomenology of the Self* (Princeton University Press/ Bollingen Foundation, 1969).

C. G. Jung excerpt describing "anima type" and excerpt describing anima as archetype: see C. G. Jung, *The Development of Personality* (Princeton University Press/Bollingen Foundation, 1954).

Excerpt describing Maria Moltzer as model for Jung's own anima: see Deirdre Bair, *Jung: A Biography* (Little Brown, 2003).

Excerpts from letters between C. G. Jung and Sigmund Freud regarding

Sabina Spielrein: see William McGuire, ed., *The Freud/Jung Letters: Abridged Edition* (Princeton University Press, 1974).

Goddess quiz and excerpts about my inner goddess, Persephone: see Jennifer Barker Woolger and Roger J. Woolger, *The Goddess Within: A Guide to the Eternal Myths that Shape Women's Lives* (Ballantine Books, 1987).

Chapter 5. Relationship

Excerpts from Sigmund Freud's letter to Jung regarding bookshelf noise and C. G. Jung excerpt about his "polygamous components": see William McGuire, ed., *The Freud/Jung Letters: Abridged Edition* (Princeton University Press, 1974).

Excerpts and descriptions of synchronicity throughout chapter: see C. G. Jung, *Synchronicity: An Acausal Connecting Principle* (Princeton University Press, 1973).

Description of Jung's relationship with Toni Wolff; Franz Jung quotation regarding his father's polygamy; C. G. Jung quotation blaming his anima; and quotation regarding Jung considering suicide: see Deirdre Bair, *Jung: A Biography* (Little Brown, 2003).

Chapter 6. The Shadow

Gary Toub and Adolf Guggenhul-Craig excerpts on the nature of the shadow: see Connie Zweig and Jeremiah Abrams, eds., *Meeting the Shadow: The Hidden Power of the Dark Side of Human Nature* (Jeremy P. Tarcher/ Penguin, 1991).

C. G. Jung excerpt on becoming conscious of the shadow and excerpt on the nature of projection: see C. G. Jung, *Aion: Researches into the Phenomenology of the Self* (Princeton University Press/Bollingen Foundation, 1969).

C. G. Jung excerpt about how "everyone carries a shadow": see C. G. Jung, *Psychology and Religion* (Yale University Press, 1960).

Chapter 7. The Ally

Description of Jung's interest in circles as symbols of the Self: see C. G. Jung et al., *Man and His Symbols* (Aldus Books Limited, 1964).

Description of ancient shamanistic practices: see Mircea Eliade, *Shamanism: Archaic Techniques of Ecstasy* (Bollingen Foundation, 1964).

Description of Blake being contacted by a supernatural being: see Stephen K. Witty, "Hearing the Voice of God: A Phenomenological Investigation," a diploma thesis for the Inter-Regional Society of Jungian Analysts (Nathrop, Colorado, 1999).

Chapter 8. Individuation

Excerpt regarding Jung's definition of individuation: see C. G. Jung, *Psychological Types* (Princeton University Press/Bollingen Foundation, 1971).

Maria-Louise von Franz excerpts on alchemy: see Marie-Louise von Franz, *Alchemical Active Imagination* (Shambhala Publication/C. G. Jung Foundation Books, 1997).

Scene about transference from Naomi Watts film: see *Ellie Parker* (2005).

C. G. Jung excerpt on transference: see C.G. Jung, *The Psychology of Transference* (Princeton University Press, 1969).

Sigmund Freud excerpt on countertransference: see Peter Gay, ed., "Observations on Transference-Love," in *The Freud Reader* (W. W. Norton, 1989).

Excerpt explaining lack of boundaries in early Jungian scene: see Deirdre Bair, *Jung: A Biography* (Little Brown, 2003).

C. G. Jung excerpt about "The serious problems in life": see C. G. Jung, *The Structure and Dynamics of the Psyche* (Princeton University Press/ Bollingen Foundation, 1970).

Arnold Mindell excerpt on death fantasies: see Arnold Mindell, *Dreambody: The Body's Role in Revealing the Self* (Sigo Press, 1982).